A Life in Balance

Finding Meaning in a Chaotic World

Charles R. Stoner
Jennifer Robin

UNIVERSITY PRESS OF AMERICA,® INC.
Lanham • Boulder • New York • Toronto • Oxford

Copyright © 2006 by
University Press of America,® Inc.
4501 Forbes Boulevard
Suite 200
Lanham, Maryland 20706
UPA Acquisitions Department (301) 459-3366

PO Box 317
Oxford
OX2 9RU, UK

Library of Congress Control Number: 2006928031
ISBN-13: 978-0-7618-3546-2 (paperback : alk. paper)
ISBN-10: 0-7618-3546-6 (paperback : alk. paper)

Contents

Preface

Does work seem to dominate your life? Are you working more but enjoying it less? Do you have a gnawing sense that life could and should be better? Are you searching for greater fulfillment, significance, and meaning? Are you simply looking for a better sense of balance in your life?

If you have identified with any of the above questions, you are not alone. Life balance is one of the more profound themes that is gripping today's society and the topic has sparked lively debate and roused research interests for the past two decades.

Unfortunately, recent evidence offers a frightening view of contemporary life balance.

- Over the last 35 years, the average American work year has increased by 200 hours, counter to the general decline in hours on the job in all other industrialized countries.
- 93% of adults agree that they are too focused on working and making money and not enough on family and community.
- 2/3 of parents with children report that they are "dissatisfied with the balance between their job and home life."
- And perhaps most telling, 75% of workers indicate that they wish they could "have a more meaningful personal life."

In the face of this evidence and the deep personal concerns behind the evidence, there is hope. Life balance can be affected and enhanced. We can have successful, rewarding careers and still experience richly textured, meaningful lives. This book examines the theme of life balance and builds a path for the realization of life balance and fulfillment.

We know and share, through first-hand experience, the penetrating struggle of working in a maze of ever-escalating demands. Seasoned mid-career executives ponder their selected paths and silently wonder if wise choices have been made. Younger managers see the shattered hopes and collateral damage of their leaders—their career role models—and yearn for something else, something more, and something different. They hope for something that will offer a greater sense of significance. There is confusion and there are questions of balance.

Against this backdrop, it is not surprising that the business world is saturated with programs and initiatives designed to ameliorate the level of work-life imbalance. Wonderful options, such as longer paid holidays, more time off for legitimate family demands, more sabbaticals and mini-sabbaticals, and greater flexibility in the formal working routine (to name just a few) are encountered. Further, research has helped clarify both the causes and effects of life-balance breakdowns. But these works, largely, have not addressed the deeper, more personal sense of imbalance that managers and professionals know and feel. And none really speak to the day-in and day-out struggles that consume managers' time and energy. Accordingly, the purpose of this book is to help busy managers and professionals find the meaning and significance they desire in their lives.

The foundations and recommendations of this book were drawn from a variety of sources. As academics and as concerned practitioners, we began with the best research and writing on the topic of balance. As we have jokingly expressed to our students, "When all else fails, turn to the data." The data clarify, guide, debunk, and provide insight and opportunity. Themes and possibilities emerge. We value the data and appreciate the need to carefully peel back layers of the topic through rigorous investigative inquiry. Yet, we understand that answers to the perplexing concerns of personal life balance will not reside fully in these investigations.

Consequently, we have reviewed and applied classic works from the fields of psychology, sociology, philosophy, business, and spirituality that were most relevant to the themes of life balance and meaning. Our impressions were guided from all directions—Frankl, Kofodimos, Hochchild, Merton—to name but a few.

Additionally, our insights were drawn from a series of interviews conducted over a six-month time period. Participants included individual managers and professionals (ranging in age from their late 20's to late 50's and from first-level professional positions through CEO), as well as 20 managerial couples (each member of the couple was interviewed independently). This base of semi-structured interviews allowed us to probe specific areas and gain detailed perspective.

Finally, our approach to life balance has been tested in a series of workshops and coaching encounters over the last three years. As such, we've seen "how it plays" with a managerial population. The ideas, questions, concerns, and open sharing of these organizational participants helped us project a realistic, practical, and frank tone throughout the book and helped us fine-tune our thinking.

Throughout the book, a number of examples and personal cases are used. We believe these examples enrich the book by offering practical and recognizable experiences. In all cases, the people referenced are individuals with whom we have worked. In most cases, they either have been participants in our research studies (which have included in-depth interviews), participants in our workshops, or men and women who have worked with us in a coaching relationship. In all cases, we have sought to offer meaningful examples while protecting identities. For this reason, names have either been omitted or pseudonyms have been used. Additionally, only broad descriptive references to their respective organizations have been provided. In some cases, composites have been created to assure the richness of the examples while protecting the identities of the respondents. Finally, in cases where we quote participants, permission has been granted.

There are a number of people to acknowledge and thank. First, we are indebted to the countless managers and professionals who have shared with us and have helped shape the eventual framework and message of this book. Not only were their comments pivotal, but their questions prompted our thinking and pushed us toward realistic answers. We'd like to thank Dr. Lori Russell-Chapin for her contributions during the early stages of the project. We are grateful to Dr. John F. Gillgan, Chairman Emeritus of Fayette Companies. Jack is one the brightest and most creative minds we know and his thoughtful reviews of our work were sources of insight. To Rob Kenny, our editor, we offer thanks for your positive reaction to our work and your attentive improvements to our final written product.

Thanks to Mary Ardapple and the folks at Apple's Bakery, and Ashley, Dallas, and the amazing staff at One World Eats and Treats. Many an oatmeal raisin muffin and spiced chai were consumed while writing and we became permanent fixtures at both of these Peoria landmarks!

Finally, we would each like to offer our special appreciation to family, colleagues, and friends who have offered steady support throughout the course of this project. For Chuck, I'd like to thank Dr. Julie Stoner, whose scholarly perspective is only eclipsed by her understanding, encouragement, and love. As with all projects, I appreciate the environment of support of my colleagues at Bradley University, particularly Dr. Sandra Perry, my department chair, and Dr. Rob Baer, my dean. Finally, thanks to Jen. The creative sessions, workshops, and writing have been stimulating and fun. I've appreciated your intelligence, insights, and energy.

As for Jennifer, first and foremost, I extend my appreciation to my coauthor, Chuck Stoner, for his dedication and commitment to this work. Of all of the projects on which we've collaborated, this is my favorite. Thank you for your support, confidence, and encouragement through my own journey toward balance. My gifts and purpose are clearer to me thanks to you. Thanks also to my family (Mom, Dad, and Katie) and friends, who have provided me personal support during this precious time. Special acknowledgements go to Stacy McManus and Michael Young, two of the most amazing people on the planet.

Part One

Chapter One

Just Above the Tree Line

*It was a clear, cool morning. A new day's sun cast patterns of color over
Conchu Lake, just off the North Kawishi River in the Minnesota boundary waters. The only sound was that of paddles, smoothly and efficiently guiding a
canoe through the water. There was not another soul in sight, and it was likely
none would be seen. Just a canoe, fishing tackle, two men, no words—both of
us immersed in and captivated by the beauty and amazement of nature's won-
derland.*

*Alan, steering from behind, offered a gentle command, "Look, over on your
right." We sat in silence as a family of otters progressed through some sort of
ritual. We edged in for a closer look, thoroughly entertained as seven tiny
heads suddenly dropped beneath the surface. Seconds passed, and then, perhaps ten yards from the focus of our attention, a single otter popped up and
beckoned us to follow. We obliged, and the pattern was repeated. We knew
what was happening; we had ventured too close and we were now being led
away to protect the family.*

*In the simplicity of the moment, two men began a rare conversation, a con-
versation about work, family, and life. We talked about what we do, why we
do it, and what really matters. Little was held back. We shared frustrations
and dreams, hoping that the lines dangling in the water would not break this
spiritual connection with an expectant tug. We spent the better part of the
morning and afternoon ostensibly fishing on that lake before heading back to
our home camp and families. We didn't catch a fish. It was perfect.*

For anyone who cared to inquire as to what we had been doing, the answer
was simple. We were fishing. Yet, fishing was merely the context for a rich
and impacting experience. The conversation was one of reflection and depth,
driving to the core of who I was and what I cherished. Indeed, my sense of

purpose, my gifts, and my life's meaning was clearer to me that day than they had been in some time. An ordinary day had been transformed into a defining moment, a unique time of sheer simplicity and honesty. And I experienced a sense of awareness, calmness, and serenity that was all too rare and fleeting.

You too have had these moments. Hopefully, they have been grasped and cherished, because what makes these experiences so special and unique is that they stand in dramatic contrast to the rapid-fire blur of events and demands that normally consume our time and energy. Let me tell you about a second day, one that occurred only a few weeks after returning from the boundary waters.

Plagued by a pressing project, I found myself wide awake at 3 am, my mind buzzing with ideas. Knowing there was no likelihood of turning off the mental whirl and returning to sleep, getting up and working seemed the most plausible option. The next 90 minutes was a time of amazing creativity and productivity. Realizing that the day had now officially started, a time of reading and reflection followed, as did a spirited early morning run. All of this before breakfast! By 8:30 am, I was working with the management team of a fast-growth organization. Our exchanges were open and frank and forward-looking. Then lunch with my college-aged son, always special. Preparation for and engagement in an active class of undergraduate students followed. This left about an hour for reviewing some research and doing some writing. I met my wife at our favorite, cozy Italian restaurant, one where the wine selections are as special as the seafood linguine. By 8:30 pm, I'm back home— exhausted from the day's activities.

What a contrast in days between this latest one and the day on the lake in the boundary waters. It is important to look carefully at these two days. Which day seems to make the stronger case for balance?

For many, the knee-jerk response is to point to the boundary waters day — a day of admitted serenity and contentment. Frankly, the boundary waters day was relaxing and fun and rejuvenating. But I'm not sure I'd call it a day when I experienced "balance." I'm also not sure how many of those days I could take before I'd be itching for something more. You see, the second day, harried though it was, provided me an opportunity to stretch my gifts and feel life's purpose. The day allowed me to have meaningful personal time, time for attending to my interests in running and fitness, the opportunity to use my talent creatively to help an organization of young leaders, the gift of working with an engaged group of students, and opportunities to have some valued "talk time" with my family. Each critical arena of my life had been engaged.

At the end of the day, I was exhausted, but I was also fulfilled and satisfied that the day had been enriching and meaningful. From my personal perspective, it certainly felt like a balanced day.

There is a common myth of balance that asserts that balance is about achieving a state of serenity and contentment.[1] We disagree. Balance is really about expressing who you are, using your gifts, living your purpose, and feeling fulfilled.

Whether on a trip similar to that in the boundary waters, or a day in which the important aspects of your life have been served, you too have experienced glimmers of who you really are. These glimmers come in seemingly inconsequential moments. They come when your colleague has to interrupt your engaged focus upon the strategic plan you are creating to ask you to lunch. They come when you watch your child reading a book and realize how similar her facial expression is to your own. A glimmer may occur when you see a kitchen light in your neighborhood switch on at 6 a.m., and you find yourself looking forward to returning to the comfort and solace of your own home after you finish your morning run. In these fleeting moments, you may be unaware of the contrast effect that often clues us to the fact that there is another way of being in the world. Or, you may consciously choose to ignore these messages. Yet, it is hard to ignore the guilt, incompleteness, and unease that accompany our return from these moments into what we may deem "real life." It is these feelings of guilt, incompleteness, and unease that have become known as a life out of balance. Times in which we are neither in touch with nor the embodiment of who we really are serve as a stark contrast to those times in which we are. We long to return to the sense of oneness, the sense that who we are and what we do are one in the same.

Many of us realize that we are somewhat off-track and "out of whack" as we pursue an elusive sense of balance. The data is compelling. Recent research shows us that the majority of American workers (55%) feel "overwhelmed by how much they have to do."[2] Nine out of ten adults (93%) agree that "they are too focused on working and making money and not enough on family and community."[3] Similarly, two of every three workers wish they could "work significantly fewer hours."[4] And perhaps more discouraging and shocking, while 80% of survey respondents are unhappy with their work-life balance, the majority of people do not believe that work-life balance is even possible.[5]

Recently, the CEO of a successful mid-sized business expressed his challenge to us during a workshop. Compelled by his organization's lofty growth targets to expand his 60-hour work week, disrupted by his wife's recent return to the corporate world, and pressed by the needs of his three teenaged children, he struggled to find "the answer" to his increasingly hectic and fragmented sense of the world. He argued that he needed more time, and he pleaded for a system or a method or unique solution of how to make it all work. He wanted it all and lived with the conviction that it could happen. To him, balance was the capacity to capture and orchestrate all the pieces so nothing was damaged or dismissed. He attended our workshop intent on investing a couple precious hours from his day and leaving with the latest 10-step solution. His hopes would not be met and his frustration would not be relieved.

You see, his view of balance, which is shared by many of the people we have worked with and interviewed, draws on traditional, formulaic conceptions. In this conception, balance suggests equity, and we attempt to attain balance by focusing our efforts on equality and equalization. Accordingly, balance requires effort if not struggle to arrange the pieces of our lives in a certain way. The quest for balance becomes a grand juggling assignment. If we are sufficiently skilled and adept, all the pieces can be kept in play. In this world of doing more, though, we have several pieces of life to juggle, and sometimes these pieces seem disjointed if not diametrically opposed. Further, missing or dropping any piece is not only discouraging, but an indication of failure. Even our language reflects this failing. How often have we heard: "She dropped the ball," or "He let that one slip between the cracks."

Let's press a bit more deeply on this point. We all have a need for the pieces to fit together. We don't like the disparate tugs and strains of competing demands. We want to service every demand, and we want to achieve a consistent approach for managing our lives, even though we are convinced that most people, at an intuitive level, realize that such a goal is fundamentally an illusion.

If it is not clear to you at this point, rest assured we intend to upend popular notions of life balance. Accordingly, we ask tough questions. What if there are no pieces to juggle? What if we are whole people and the pieces are simply an illusion borne of the words we choose when describing success? In our business vernacular, we use the word "balance" rather cavalierly, without examining the assumptions behind it. In order to have a full and complete life, should all of our energy, our time, and our accomplishments within a work setting be balanced by equal amounts of energy, time, and accomplishment in non-work settings? Must the accomplished corporate leader's life be viewed as sad and empty if she does not also have a beautiful family and a rich spiritual life? Should the stay-at-home parent's existence be seen as a noble sacrifice of more public accomplishment? If you are to be in balance, must your life be partitioned, and must all the parts be structured in a very calculating and precise manner? Note how counter all this is to the magical experience in the boundary waters or the excitement of a rich, full day.

Thus, we argue that a different conceptualization of balance is in order, one that carries different assumptions. We disagree that the complex and disturbing feelings that most successful professionals feel can be fully captured by labeling them an issue of "balance." And we cringe at the actions most take once that label is applied—expending exorbitant amounts of effort to rearrange the surface area of our lives in hopes that a new arrangement will allow us to more fully express who we are at our core.

We will argue throughout this book that the experience of balance hinges on an understanding of personal fulfillment and significance. We know from experience that these themes often strike terror in the hearts of seasoned business people. These themes may seem more appropriate for the realms of philosophy and theology. These themes beg the great questions and the great quandaries of the ages.

Here, we extend a call to acknowledge that balance is not an equality issue, nor is it perfecting a day-to-day routine. Likewise, balance is not really a time issue or even an energy issue. Balance is more fully a meaning issue. Let's not gloss over this crucial point, one that is the essence of our conceptualization of balance: *Balance is a meaning issue.*

Meaning is intensely personal. Even if it could be captured in words, it is not possible to do so universally. The issue of meaning is one that has been considered historically by academics and philosophers alike, and the only conclusion we may draw from their work is that any definition of meaning is elusive, if not impossible. Victor Frankl, in his seminal work *Man's Search for Meaning*, never in fact defines the term. Rather, he says: "What matters, therefore, is not the meaning of life in general but rather the specific meaning of a person's life at a given moment."[6] Each moment, we argue, has meaning to the extent that the individual expresses his or her core self. Therefore, it is the act of creating balance or meaning by expressing one's core self, perhaps better deemed "balancing," that we are concerned with in this book.

At the core, each individual possesses both purpose and gifts. One's purpose is that deep personal sense of unique significance. Purpose is what provides us worth and meaning. Consequently, one's own purpose can never be fulfilled by another because it requires a certain constellation of characteristics, life experiences, and skills that are inimitable. And, incidentally, the constellation of characteristics, life experiences, and skills comprise one's gifts, the other key component of the core self. Balancing, then, is creating situations in which one's gifts and purpose are aligned with one's life situation.

In Part Two of this book, we provide examples, thought provoking questions, and recommendations to derive meaning through balancing, to experience oneness and significance on a more consistent basis by assuring your actions and activities are aligned with your gifts and purpose. Part One is dedicated to more fully exploring the epidemic of imbalance, understanding balance from both a historical and contextual perspective, and reorienting the reader's conceptualization of a life in balance.

The work-life balance literature is rich and informative, and we intend to summarize and discuss it next with respect and deference. But, we also intend to point out where the literature has led us, all of us—you, your organization, your employees, and coworkers alike—astray in search of obtaining the ever-elusive balance. Make no mistake, as seen in the alarming, disheartening, and shocking research findings and anecdotes we see every day, what we are currently doing in service of obtaining balance is not working.

But first, a metaphor. As avid hikers, we have experienced the exhilaration of the climb, attacking a mountain and making the steep ascent. As the air thins, the entire landscape begins to change. The rich collage of foliage becomes sparse and we are able to see what was hidden from view only feet earlier. Just above the tree line, it all looks different, somehow clearer and more fundamental. Just above the tree line, we are also able to look down to see the forest that was once hidden by the trees. We see the complexities, the patterns with fresh eyes and new perspective. And so it is with the topic of balance. Just above the tree line, in the space between the density of real life and the thin air of our idealized summit, we realize that there must be a better path.

ANOTHER LOOK BEFORE YOU LEAP

We conclude this chapter, as we will each chapter in the book, with questions and commentary we have received from workshop participants and individuals we have coached. These are women and men who are working to reach their personal "better path" toward balance. They ask one last question or make a crucial comment in our workshops before they take those critical first steps (that may, for many, look like a leap).

During a large public workshop, we received the following reaction:

> "I like your definition of balance and balancing. In many respects it's freeing. I don't have to feel guilty . . . because I actually enjoy what I'm doing. It might not appear balanced to someone else, but to me it's a harmonious mixture of activity that is fulfilling and interesting . . . Maybe I'm not crazy after all."

This woman, a successful professional in her early 40's, even confided that friends and colleagues had chastised her "workaholic" ways. She admitted that her life was a whirl of activity, replete with work, community involvements, friends, travel, and frequent doses of personal escape. Truly, there was little down time. Yet she cherished each of her life's activities. She found strength and significance in each endeavor and she felt fulfillment.

Her pattern of constant action may not be for everybody. This pattern may even prove too exhausting for this woman ten years from now. But we agree with her that she needs to be "freed" from the cultural notion that something is wrong with the pace she now finds so meaningful and purposeful. There is also a deeper dimension working here. Her formidable talents are being expressed and enhanced as she lives, no doubt contributing to the sense of meaning she describes.

This example underscores the personally attuned, idiosyncratic nature of balance. The example also provides a great view of reframing assumptions that will be a feature of this book.

NOTES

1. We found this perception of serenity and contentment in our original research for this book. While respondents knew the experience of imbalance, they had difficulty explaining the concept of balance. Accordingly, they resorted, at least initially, to more simplistic "contentment" arguments. Fortunately, further probing in our interviews helped the participants move beyond their initial explanations to uncover complex and realistic levels of depth. Even well articulated arguments suggest at least one perspective of balance occurs when there is a conflict or interference between life roles. For example, see Michael R. Frone, J.C. Quick, L.E. Tetrick, "Work-Family Balance," *Handbook of Occupational Psychology* (Washington, D.C.: American Psychological Association, 2003): 143–62.

2. Research reported by Ellen Galinsky, Stacy S. Kim, and James T. Bond, *Feeling Overworked: When Work Becomes Too Much* (New York: Families and Work Institute, 2001).

3. Results of a 2004 poll conducted for the Center for a New American Dream and reported by Sarah Roberts, "Survey Confirms that Americans are Overworked,Overspent, and Rethinking the American Dream," *The New American Dream 2005* http://www.newdream.org/newlsletter/survey.php> (31 January 2005).

4. Families and Work Insitute, *The 1997 National Study of the Changing Workforce* (New York: Families and Work Institute, 1998), 8.

5. Results of a Survey reported in "Failing at the Balancing Act," *Computing Canada* 30, issue 17 (November 26, 2004): 10.

6. Victor E. Frankl, *Man's Search for Meaning* (New York: Simon & Schuster, 1984), 113.

Chapter Two

Dazed and Confused

On September 14, 2004, Doug Farrell faced his board of directors and announced that he was stepping down as President. The board members, many of whom were close associates who had worked with Doug for years, were awed by the shocking news. In retrospect, there had been signs. But in the flurry of business activities, they did not see it coming.

Neither did most of his executive team or his employees. They knew Doug as a 45 year old, energetic and outgoing leader, who had scrapped and fought his way to the top. A natural leader, seemingly comfortable in his role, they were at a loss to explain the news.

The decision had not come easily for Doug. A bright underachiever in college, Doug hit his stride in law school. Graduating in the top quarter of his class, he accepted a job at a fast growing, highly competitive service organization. His goal from the beginning was to reach the top before he was 40. With the support of a strong family and paced by an aggressive travel schedule, his talents as a salesman and negotiator were soon recognized by upper management. More challenging assignments came his way, the travel intensified, the money poured in, and a fast-track set of promotions fueled his enthusiasm. He could deliver a compelling motivational speech to employees or schmooze with Fortune 500 executives, all with apparent ease, confidence, and success.

There were some who were surprised that three senior executives were passed over in favor of Doug. He heard the comments and understood the tone of cynicism. He was two months shy of his 40th birthday and the presidential office was now his. Of course, his relative youth and the unsettling lack of total acceptance by some in the business prodded him to work longer and harder. He had never experienced a significant personal failure in his life and this would not be the first. Throughout the entire experience, he remained closely dedicated to his family, and his three children enjoyed their turns of occasionally joining him for some of his travels. By all accounts, his family relationships remained strong and encouraging.

Even today, over two years after his decision, Doug is hard-pressed to offer a compelling explanation. "It just didn't seem right anymore. I didn't like what I was becoming. Even little sacrifices started to bother me. It's confusing, but I just had to step in a different direction."

The evidence is clear and irrefutable. Over the past 35 years, Americans, particularly those in managerial and professional positions, are working more. Americans spent an average of 163 hours more per year on the job in 1987 than they did in 1969.[1] That's roughly adding an extra month to the work year over a period just shy of 20 years. And the trend appears to continue. According to the United Nations International Labor Organization, U.S. workers "added 36 hours to their average work year during the 1990s . . ."[2] In less than four decades, we've increased our work year by nearly 200 hours.

Even more striking is that this surge in work runs counter to the general decline in hours at work experienced by all other industrialized countries.[3] At some point, we are caught in the dilemma framed by Joanne Ciulla, "How did we get from the idea that we work to live to the idea that we live to work?"[4]

Unrelenting schedules and workloads leave us dazed and confused. Why has a work-dominated lifestyle become so common, so expected, and so accepted? Why has pervasive work involvement become such a striking reality for contemporary managers and professionals? In reviewing the literature, four main themes of reasoning or explanation emerge. People are more enmeshed in work due to (1) increased organizational pressure; (2) career pressure; (3) compensatory work efforts to reduce life imbalance; and (4) heightened aspirations to accomplish personal goals. These four themes become even more intriguing as we realize that for any given individual, a complex interaction or combination of these themes is likely at play. Let's take a careful look at each line of reasoning.

THE ORGANIZATIONAL PRESSURE ARGUMENT

Pragmatists take a direct route in explaining the work-hours explosion, noting that it is driven, at least in part, by growing organizational pressures to reduce costs and enhance productivity.[5] Organizations are operating leaner than ever, largely in an effort to reduce labor costs. To an extent, outsourcing has been utilized as a mechanism for paring down while retaining service and efficiency. Yet, let's be realistic. In most cases, streamlining strategies place additional demands on each remaining worker. Not only are fewer people being asked to meet expanding requirements, but accompanying mandates for efficiency and timeliness create a context where it is nearly impossible to succeed without employees putting in additional hours at work. "Do more with less" is the contemporary competitive mantra. Understandably, each individual worker feels the pressure to increase hours at work as a logical route for reaching an ever-escalating set of organizational demands.

There is a related organizational pressure. Often, long work hours become expected and valued as signals of dedication, commitment, and loyalty.[6] Further, as competitive pressures intensify, professionals and knowledge workers are expected to demonstrate their organizational support through a focused drive to work as long as necessary to assure goal attainment.[7]

We see this pressure as a dominant theme, present in nearly every workshop or intervention we have with today's leaders. The pressure is prevalent among emerging leaders in their late twenties, thirties and forties whose focus is complicated by young families and burgeoning careers. These leaders tell us that "finding more time" is the toughest issue and biggest problem they face. Their voices are not alone. More senior leaders, with their own set of familial issues (not the least of which is responsibilities toward aging parents), indicate that they'd like to "slow down just a bit." But, they realize that they cannot. Indeed, the surging organizational pressure to do more is without generational boundaries.

Herein lays a paradox. While organizational efforts at becoming more efficient pay off in the form of profits and competitive advantage, individual workers often feel depleted and overwhelmed in the process. Of course leaders and professionals are generally bright people who readily understand the pressures driving organizational action. They recognize the demands of a shifting, complicated, competitive landscape. Conceptually and intellectually, it all makes good business sense.

But they are far more than intellectual beings. At the personal, gut-level, they feel cheated, manipulated, and taken for granted—pawns in a broader, corporate game. A painful sense of loss ensues, one in which the expectation of being treated fairly and humanely by the organization is called into question. Realize that this questioning is rarely verbalized to organizational decision-makers. To do so would signal either weakness or a perception of disloyalty or both. Further, such questioning would be an act of irrationality given that the worker, at least intellectually, understands the competitive pressures prompting escalating work demands.

With organizational logic and personal intensity clashing, what are we to do? We have found that it is common for professionals to recognize and even justify the organizational response rather than explore their own gut-level reactions. Accordingly, the personal impact registers an internalized sense of loss, as emotional signals are driven beneath the surface. Realize that the process of internalization is a psychological attempt to minimize felt emotions, attempting to render these emotions to be non-existent or at least non-apparent. And, once the emotions cease to exist at a conscious level, the organization's line of competitive reasoning "wins out." Consequently, rational, non-emotive workers put in additional hours because they understand the "logic" of the underlying organizational pressures. There is nothing else to consider from the individual's point of view.

Our attempt here is not to offer a scathing thumping or indictment of corporate America. The pattern noted above may not be the organizational intent. But it is the outcome. And, it is an outcome that cannot be upheld for any length of time before the repressed sense of loss and grief springs forth, manifested in emotion and action.

Let's dig even a bit deeper. At times, the organizationally-driven theme for increased individual workloads centers on powerful, unwritten, behind-the-scenes dynamics. For example, consider the impact of corporate downsizing. Part of the myriad issues that downsizing survivors face is the "am I next?" thinking.[8] This threat prompts one to press on harder and longer, in a vain attempt to prove one's indispensability to the organization, thereby minimizing the likelihood of redundancy. Strategically, survivors work to reduce the threat of vulnerability that comes from being an "expendable" worker in an organization bent on slashing labor costs.

Ciulla astutely refers to this as "the work ethic of fear."[9] People no longer work for the joy of reward or the satisfaction of accomplishment. Instead, they work to avoid a negative consequence, which means that they are willing to put in excessive time and effort that actually depletes their effectiveness and well-being. Fear drives people to take on activities that would be out of the question under different circumstances. As a mid-level manager who was interviewed for one of our studies put it, "I want better balance. But right now with all the restructuring, I dare not cut back or show even a slight tendency to pull back at work." It is not only downsizing that creates such determination. There is also a very general sense of career pressure driving workers to new levels of commitment and productivity.

THE CAREER PRESSURE ARGUMENT

Even if competitive organizational pressures are low, many professionals escalate their work commitment because they view heavy work involvement as a competitive edge leading to recognition and advancement in today's streamlined organizational world. Listen to the reasoning, expressed below by the president of a large service organization:

"Balance is a very important and admirable concept, but like most things worth-while, I always found it difficult to achieve. In fact as a younger working pro-fessional, I am not even sure I recognized that such a thing existed or there was a need for it. I can remember being totally focused on my career. . . . Balance or the lack thereof, sometimes is the competitive edge, if you will, that a person can have in competing for promotions."

He further acknowledged that he was quite conscious of his current junior executives who put in long hours and those who did not; admitting that he viewed the former group with considerably more respect and advancement potential than the latter group.

Again, logic prevails. As organizations have become flatter, fewer promo-tional opportunities exist. Competition for key projects, plum assignments, and challenging growth opportunities has never been more intense. A per-sonal ethic of work dominance, with an unflinching commitment to "give your all" for the business, can provide a differentiation from the masses. At the least, a failure to comply with a strong work ethic will, in most cases, send the wrong signals and potentially stall career advancement.

Consider another take on this theme, this time from a general manager of a mid-sized media firm:

"There's nothing magic about 40 (a 40-hour work week). I don't know who made that up. . . . Two people hire at the same time, the same qualifications, the same talent, and they work for somebody for two years. One of them works 40 hours a week and never misses a day. The other works 60 hours a week and never misses a day. The 60 hours a week guy now has 3 years experience based on the way we measure everything against a 40 hour week. . . . You can't get [experience] except through time. So if you're doing 60 hours a week and some-one else is doing 40, you just picked up 50% more experience."

He asserts what many hard-driving, success-oriented professionals believe. If one works longer and harder, a "leg up" on rivals vying for a limited array of upper-tier leadership slots is gained. To the extent that professionals hold-ing this view are also vocal organizational leaders, workers hungry for ad-vancement get the message loud and clear: "Work. Work a lot." Richard Donkin has argued that "the work ethic seems to be buried as deeply within Western society as the chemical reaction that pumps us adrenaline in the event of sudden danger." He notes that this work ethic is so ingrained that "some of us are psychologically incapable of easing up."[10]

In sum, both organizational and career pressures arguments amount to this: people work more in order to maximize organizational and personal prosper-ity. These are not aberrant actions. There is logic and rationality behind them.

However, in speaking with managers and professionals in the course of our work, it is clear to us that these are not the only reasons for increased work intensity. There are other factors at play, factors that are pervasive and complex in explaining chronic imbalance. Compensatory work efforts and heightened personal aspirations are these factors, and they are discussed next.

COMPENSATORY WORK EFFORT ARGUMENT

The compensatory work effort argument is markedly different than the pressure-based arguments above. It states that some people *choose* to work more in a valiant attempt to reduce feelings of life discomfort. As such, work becomes a mechanism of compensation, an attempt to counteract or neutralize missing foundations of balance. Not surprisingly, increased efforts at work often completely overshadow other areas of life; the most often reported being time with family and physical health. Although seemingly illogical behavior, there are reasonable explanations for these compensatory actions.

The first explanation comes from the work of social researcher Arlie Hochchild who argued that some people actually seek additional time at work because of the tension, uncertainty, and lack of fulfillment they experience at home.[11] For these people, work provides structure and predictability. In short, Hochchild argues that many people spend more and more time at work because they want to do so, finding the work environment more supportive, controllable, and comfortable than their home alternatives.

We saw this pattern in our research, with a number of participants reporting that they plunged themselves into their work and took solace in the "refuge" of work as their marital conditions were in the throes of deterioration. Additionally, our research suggested that the pattern extended even further than that noted by Hochchild. For example, professionals described intensifying their work activities as they became less secure about changing family responsibilities and relationships, damaged friendships, and even during intense periods of personal uncertainty. Although one may be tempted to label this intensification of work as a form of escape for the situations noted above, the term compensation is more accurate. Many people have told us that when things were "falling apart" in their lives, work was something they could "get their hands around," something they knew "they could do well."

Let's look carefully at one successful executive who had taken this compensatory approach when faced with life imbalance. A manager in his early 40s with two young children and a supportive spouse who made the choice to stay home to raise the children, Phil reported spending close to 11 hours per day at work. He often arrived home just in time to see the kids before they went to bed. but this precious time with them also was infected with thoughts of work. Time in the evenings with his spouse was often fraught with arguments and tense reviews of social and household obligations that were not being met. Weekends were usually dedicated to these obligations and to spending time together as a family. Yet Phil could not seem to bring himself to enjoy these times without feeling guilty that he had been what he perceived to be an absentee father throughout the week.

His solution: work more. If he arrived home after the kids went to bed, he did not have to experience thoughts competing for his attention, thoughts of his kids and his work. If he spent less time with his spouse, he would not have to face her tears about not only failing in his obligations, but in her missing his presence in her life. He was beginning to believe that he was not cut out to be a good spouse, or a good parent, which, not surprisingly, led to the urge to work even more at a job in which he felt a great deal of accomplishment and success.

We agreed with Phil that his home life was not fulfilling, but communicated that this may be due to his self-imposed avoidance of a very important part of his life. It was not that his family was unimportant to him, but that it was of the utmost importance. We encouraged him to reflect upon his life's purpose in the roles of spouse and parent, and to acknowledge his feelings of frustration, guilt, and shame surrounding his absence in his family's life. We are not naïve. This is an unpleasant undertaking. However, when we see successful professionals working more due to feeling work is a more structured and rewarding environment, we encourage them to ask themselves why this is the case. Taking responsibility for a home life that has become anything other than a supportive haven that recharges a manager after the stresses of work take hold is often the first step in reclaiming balance.

There is another compensatory explanation for why people work more, and it is in opposition to the first. People may work more not because they prefer the work environment to the home environment, but because they believe that working more will alleviate work demands and allow a return to a more equitable distribution of time between work and other areas of life. These individuals realize the importance of family and non-work endeavors, but see the only way to devote time to all facets of life is to finish work.

We call this "when this project is over" thinking. Many managers mistakenly believe that the completion of the current project will reduce the pressures felt to spend additional hours at work. Most of us realize, intuitively, the fallacy of this thinking. There is always another project, another deadline, or another crisis that must be addressed. The game simply goes on and on.

There is a final complication that must be addressed. Heightened personal aspirations affect our capacity to move off the treadmill of work. Let's look more closely at this fourth, and perhaps most insidious, line of reasoning for the increased time and attention devoted to work.

HEIGHTENED PERSONAL ASPIRATIONS

Let's face it. Successful people are typically enmeshed in a pattern of escalating achievement. Accomplishment does not satiate the desire for further accomplishment; instead, increased levels of achievement spur most of us toward even higher aspirations.

Increased time at work becomes a life style decision prompted by the comforts that more work (and accordingly, more money) provides. Former Labor Secretary Robert Reich has noted that not only are people working longer hours, but . . . "the richer you are, the more likely it is that you are putting in long and harried hours at work."[12] Reich argues that securing additional spending power makes it hard not to continue to intensify the amount of time at work. Understandably, it is much harder to contract a lifestyle that has expanded based upon increased income and resources.

It's not that simple, though. Fueling this personal drive is the fact that those who work more and accomplish more are valued more in our organizations and in our culture. This underlying philosophy is fundamental to our competitive, free enterprise model of social exchange. Consider what is often the first response to the question "Can you tell me about yourself?" We typically begin by discussing what we do, what we've achieved, and what we are working toward next. This tendency illustrates our willingness to focus upon what we've accomplished as the fundamental indicator of who we are.

At a personal level, being valued taps into our need for personal significance, arguably the most powerful individual motivator. The feeling of significance—that we count, that we're important, that we are needed, that we make a difference and have an impact—is critical to why so many of us work so hard. Social institutions such as organizations, families, and schools capitalize upon this, sometimes inadvertently. Regardless of the ultimate source of the pressure, the end result is that people become trapped in an escalating quest for significance. Often those who are most entrapped are those who are the most accomplished and achievement-oriented.

Consider the young man who is encouraged and prodded to maximize the years of his high school experience by assuming an array of activity that culminates in honor and recognition. Is it surprising that this young man demonstrates the same single-minded drive for success as he embarks on a career? Is it surprising that he marries a similar hard-charger? Is it reasonable that their children will be pushed toward even higher levels of accomplishment, ensuring not only the perpetuation but the escalation of this honored and rewarded cycle?

Thus, even though we decry imbalance, imbalance is the unwritten and unspoken means to the end of an achievement-oriented person, organization, and society. Let's not fool ourselves. We play a word and mind game at best. We condemn the vestiges of imbalance, but openly embrace the cultural foundations that propel further imbalance. Merton said it cogently, "My admiration of what I am is falsified by my admiration for what I do."[13]

And so we work. The pace increases. The demands become unrelenting. We wish there were more, there were something different. We overcompensate by trying to find this something more in our work rather than ourselves. We wish the drive would somehow end. But it does not. And it most acutely does not end for the most productive among us. We want to escape but are too ingrained to break the pattern. And so we declare that our lives are horribly out of balance. We are dazed and confused.

The Bottom Line

What does the forgoing discussion mean for those of us who are caught in the cycle of work dominance? How do pressing and ever expanding demands really affect us?

For many, the commitment and intentional desire to work more hours is coupled with a sense of personal loss for doing so. Even as time at work has escalated, 90% of workers say they never have enough time to get everything done on their jobs.[14] In a recent nationally representative poll of 1269 adults, 85% of the respondents indicated that society's priorities regarding work and non-work activities are "out of whack."[15] Over half of the respondents to a recent poll indicated that they would be more satisfied with their lives if they could spend more time with family and friends.[16]

Young workers espouse commitment to breaking the time drain paradigm of their parents. In one study, 70% reported that they would never allow their work lives to become more important than other areas and domains, most notably family and friends. Yet, evidence suggests a breach in enacting these commitments. Young college graduates contend that they want work-life balance. Yet, soon their drive for career success prompts increasingly long hours at work and an unsatisfactory assessment of the work and home connection.[17]

In an insightful recent report sponsored by the government of Canada, young parents indicated a pervasive sense of guilt for not spending enough time with their families. In fact, two-thirds of full-time employed parents with children are "dissatisfied with the balance between their job and home life."[18] In a recent study of 5500 British households who participated in the British

Household Panel Survey, 37% of men and 41% of women would prefer to work fewer hours, while only 7% of men and 4% of women would prefer to work more.[19] As if to underscore this theme, research indicates that respondents that report the highest quality of life devote more time to family.[20]

Even when organizations provide the means to help restructure life's responsibilities, employees are reluctant to take the work-life benefits offered them. According to a recent survey of human resource professionals, this view is based on the employees' belief that taking available benefits (flextime, telecommuting, etc.) would negatively affect their careers.[21]

Unfortunately, these researchers may not be considering the most serious of casualties. They are in danger of losing not only their careers, but their sense of hope.

LOST HOPE

The data reported above indicate that we are working more and enjoying it less. It is not getting better; if anything, it is getting worse. Not surprisingly, many of the men and women who have participated in our studies have demonstrated a fatalistic perspective toward balance. While it may appear harsh to suggest such a label, the desperation and pessimism these people express indicates that they see no way out of their current plight. While they wish for something better, they have little notion of what that something actually is and they express resignation that it probably won't happen anyway. Listen to the voice of this struggle, as expressed by a 42-year-old manager of a service organization:

> "That's kinda how I feel life is. It's a juggling act. You know I always swore that when my second kid came that I would still do dates with (my first child) and take out (my second child) and still not forget my spouse . . . I'm not doing a very good job at that. So I really feel life is imbalanced. . . . One of the signs is moodiness for me, and a lot of thought of death and how short life really is. My father died at 53 and I'm 42. . . ."

He remembered that he had seen what a work-dominated life had done to his father, recounting the hard driving regimen his father had followed prior to dying of heart failure, and vowing to never let that happen to him. Sadly, he admitted that in many ways the pattern was being repeated. He commented on being on that same treadmill and not knowing how to get off. He recognized his condition and the effect it had on those he loved most. Yet, there was fatalism in his voice and manner—a sort of desperate resignation. He was close to losing all hope that things would change or improve.

There are many reasons for this condition. First, as we have already mentioned, many people have gained a life style that they do not wish to sacrifice. Families enjoy the amenities that come with organizational achievement, amenities that extend beyond money to include status, social arrangements, and community connections, to name only a few. Backing away from these opportunities represents a cost many people choose not to incur.

Second, also noted earlier, most people work in organizational settings where demands and expectations are escalating not diminishing. These workers (typically upwardly mobile managers and professionals) fear that refusal to ratchet-up to meet organizational expectations will be detrimental. They fear being blackballed for exhibiting lowered corporate commitment. This label increases one's vulnerability in an age of organizational cost containment and generalized streamlining.

Third, and perhaps most pervasive, these people have defined themselves through their work and careers. As we have already indicated in Chapter One, there is nothing wrong with this unless it becomes the only base for self-realization. Of course, as career consumption marginalizes other domains of one's core self (a concept to be further explored in Chapter Seven) the likelihood of a prevailing "career-based" definition of self is increased.

Many people feel caught. They are not content with what they experience and feel, but they see no way out. In interviews they have told us, quite frankly and quite bluntly, that "backing off is not an option." We can see why a sense of hopelessness creeps in. We can also see the dangerous predicament that is being posed. Here, the stress literature provides a clue. This combined sense that things are desperate and the hopelessness that they will not get better are the foundations for stress-induced "psychological burnout."[22] Most of the people we work with are not yet there, but many are edging dangerously close.

When hope is lost, people are changed. Optimism is gone. Resiliency is shattered. Perspective is lost. And if one is to believe the research being done on emotional intelligence, one's managerial capacities and successes are severely restricted in the process.[23] The need to maintain a positive and constructive attitude in the face of adversity, which is so crucial to leadership success, is shaken.

Therefore, the pattern and line of progression that produces these feelings of hopelessness must be checked and mediated, both for the individual and in service of the severe leadership crisis we are facing in this country. But how can this be done?

Business guru Lou Tice has opined that "most of our strategies are not based on what can be but on what already is."[24] There is richness in his observation. We become so locked in a pattern of behavior that we search for answers within our established realm of thinking and behaving. The chances of creative and meaningful solutions are certainly restricted by these narrow bounds. Zander and Zander, in their best-selling work *The Art of Possibility*, offer that "many of the circumstances that seem to block us in our daily lives may only appear to do so based on a framework of assumptions we carry with us. Draw a different frame around the same set of circumstances and new pathways come into view."[25]

Recent work on the emotion of hope is most illuminating.[26] Hope arises when two conditions are met. First, one must have a goal or outcome that is desired. Second, one must believe that there exists some possibility that the outcome can be attained. This provides us the guidance we need to begin our process of reclaiming balance. That is, we must approach the problem by addressing both conditions. First, we must have a clear recognition of the outcome we seek. And second, a path of possibility must be prescribed. Indeed, those wallowing in the depths of imbalance feel lost on both of these conditions. They do not know what they want and they do not know how to get there.

Again, one can understand why there is a lack of clarity regarding the specific outcomes one desires. We hear managers tell us that "there must be more to life," that they want "deeper meaning," or that they wish to simply have a "fuller life." Such wishful thinking often lacks focus and one's range of possibilities shrinks more and more. We address these external messages, some vague and some contradictory, with greater detail in following chapters.

A CAUTIONARY PERSPECTIVE

Nearly two decades ago, Diane Fassel suggested that "work is a modern epidemic and it is sweeping our land."[27] Data indicates that the condition she described has expanded, not abated, in recent years. Yet, there is another complication—another confusing dimension.

We might conclude that Americans, lured into working more, face a single-headed monster—the insidious demands of too much work. While this argument has some merit, care must be exercised. It is too simplistic and negates the complex role work plays in our lives. We must not dismiss or shortchange the positive impact of work and we must be careful to affirm the personal importance and value of work. For most of us, work is a key force in our lives, and the significance of the work domain to overall life meaning and contentment is well established.[28]

People need to work, as evidenced by considerable study of those who are out of work. Work provides a sense of competence, a sense of utilization, and a sense of significance. Although work does not define—totally and completely—who we are, much of our self concept is linked with the work we do.

Certainly, work provides the means to satisfy life's fundamental needs. But work also taps a range of higher-level, infinite needs. Accordingly, gaining a sense of personal significance through work does not satiate the need for significance. More than likely, that taste of significance whets the appetite for more. The drive to work and the need to excel at work are reasonable and to an extent inexhaustible.

The evidence gets even more complex and complicated. In their pivotal study, *Work and Family—Allies or Enemies*, Friedman and Greenhaus pose an intriguing question. They ask if "work and family stand in opposition?" In other words, are these two important life domains "competing for time and attention, draining energy and evoking conflict?"[29] From much of our foregoing discussion, the answer appears to be yes.

However, the authors note that each sphere of life may provide meaningful and impacting experiences that enhance and enrich other parts of life. In short, their argument suggests that the domains of life can be integrative as well as conflictual.[30] Central to their research and subsequent arguments is the notion of "emotional gratification." Emotional gratification is the satisfaction we experience when either work or family fulfills important goals or needs. Accordingly, the emotional gratification we experience in one domain (say work) can directly and positively affect our emotional gratification in other domains (say family and personal life). It's important to recognize that this integrative view of work and life and the need for balance has gained popularity in recent years.

Let's think through this idea a bit more. In general, we know that work is more likely to intrude into the family domain than vice versa.[31] But must this intrusion always be diminishing and destructive? Is it conceivable that work actually could have a "positive spillover" on the family or the rest of life for that matter? Could the manager who has full and satisfying work experiences actually project a more positive and responsive attitude toward her family? Could this same manager actually have a more engaged sense of self, feeling better about and taking better care of personal needs? Or how about moving the argument around? Could the manager who has learned tolerance and understanding by handling a family crisis convert that sensitivity into the workplace? The answers are a resounding—yes!

So the plot has thickened and become more nuanced. As in any difficult intrapersonal and interpersonal exploration, questions abound and answers are guided by data, but ultimately, they are decidedly idiosyncratic. When and how does work move from a healthy, life-enhancing experience to an obsessive and destructive drain? Is that point determined by a given number of hours? Or is the point a function of the meaning derived from the work we do? Or is the point drawn from the opportunities foregone as we engage in more and more work?

Sifting through existing data and conducting our own interviews and research, we offer some conclusions. Work can be overwhelming and depleting, draining time and energy from other dimensions of life and leaving one with the sense of life imbalance. So the question becomes, "When does work become too much?"

Some efforts have tried to prescribe a target limit on the number of hours one should work. There is some interesting data here.[32] Although this data can offer important cues and benchmarks, it can easily take us in the wrong direction, suggesting a formulistic view of balance.

We take a different stance and present a counter-argument. For most of us, work becomes too much when we become so absorbed in work that our physical and psychological energy for other key areas of life is depleted. Clearly, this absorption could be time-related. But it is more importantly determined by whether work plays an energy- enhancing or energy-depleting role in our lives.

In essence, when you are confined by work activity that runs counter to or limits your capacity to use your unique gifts, work becomes draining and destabilizing. You feel underutilized. Value, meaning, and significance are on the line. This view is a bit rebellious but not at all novel. The psychological literature has long held that when one behaves "out of preference," the personal outcome is depleting and de-energizing.[33] Accordingly, when one works in a personally restrictive environment, the same type of depletion and de-energization takes place.

REALLY DAZED AND CONFUSED

Now, we are really dazed and confused. Let's review what we have said. People are working more and enjoying it less. Work can add to life's meaning and one's personal significance. But it can also drain and reduce one's full sense of life meaning. There are positive and enhancing aspects to work as well as depleting components. While the lack of time may make an otherwise enhancing experience turn into a depleting one, the assumed relationship between time and fulfillment is far from linear. This is one reason we find ourselves bewildered in the search for balance. We wish it were that straightforward and that we could simply structure our lives in order to maximize the time-fulfillment equation.

It is an interesting concept—structuring time to maximize fulfillment. However, the actions associated with structuring time in this way are not easy tasks, as many of you have already discovered. We have lost count of the number of professionals who have discovered the magical allocation of time, only to become further exhausted by attempting to follow a rigid and unyielding schedule. Life's events refuse to cooperate, and the formula meant to liberate one from imbalance becomes a straightjacket. There must be another way. In the chapters that follow and particularly in Part Two of this book, we offer a more complex explanation, but one that is less frustrating and more affirming in its execution.

Many of you are in the midst of a revolution. You are experiencing a revolution between career and family, a revolution between career and self, and a revolution that is taking you toward life's meaning. As in any important movement, the goal is clearer than the path. The path is shrouded with diversions and mixed messages. These are the foci of our next two chapters.

ANOTHER LOOK BEFORE YOU LEAP

"I understand the need for a work experience and a life experience that is full and satisfying. But given the pressures and arguments you outline, how can a talented young professional play the corporate game, win advancements, and succeed without putting in the long hours that are expected and rewarded by my company?"

This is probably a question many of you would pose. The arguments for long hours of work are convincing and they are deeply ingrained and reinforced in our organizational and social contexts. You probably want an answer that prescribes a clear path of resolution. There is none.

The intent of this chapter is to demonstrate the confusing complexity of what is being experienced. First, work is important. We all realize that work provides us with a package of pay and benefits that allow us to secure our immediate physical needs and assure their continuation into the future. Work also provides as series of intrinsic needs that allow us to experience challenge, excitement, competence, significance, and personal growth. In short, we need work—a reality we neither minimize nor trivialize.

At the same time, we see evidence of the depleting and debilitating outcomes of overwork all around us. For some people, an over-commitment to work has led them to lose perspective in life. In this scheme, purpose and meaning in life are sacrificed. That's the tipping point. That's what we want you to think about and realize and experience and admit—if it applies! If work is full (as described in the question) and if that fullness allows you to be all you are and desire to be, then work dominance is not *your* issue. However, to the extent that work crowds, obstructs, or forces deviation from your fullest sense of meaning, then appreciate that this is *your* issue. At this point, an honest personal admission is what is needed and all we ask.

So, back to the heart of the question. We would assume that since you chose to attend our workshop and ask this question, work is not providing all that you desire. That's the first critical awareness. It is an awareness many fail to admit, and it is an awareness that fewer still are able to exploit. There can be a coexistence of engaged, important work and a rich, meaningful life. But it probably won't look exactly as you have imagined or idealized it would look. It's that different, reframed look that we'll explore with you in subsequent chapters.

NOTES

1. Juliet Schor, *The Overworked American: The Unexpected Decline of Leisure* (New York: Basic Books, 1992).

2. Bettye H. Pruitt and Rhona Rapoport, *Looking Backwards to Go Forward: A Timeline of the Work-Family Field in the United States since World War II* (New York: Sloan Work and Family Resource Center, 2002).

3. Schor, *The Overworked American.*

4. Joanne B. Ciulla, *The Working Life: The Promise and Betrayal of Modern Work* (New York: Times Books, 2002): 16–17.

5. These themes are driven by a number of reports. For example, see Charles J. Hobson, Linda DeLunas, and Dawn Kesic, "Compelling Evidence of the Need for Corporate Work/Life Balance Initiatives: Results from a National Survey of Stressful Life-Events," *Journal of Employment Counseling* 38, issue 1 (March, 2001): 38–44; and Judi Casey, "Why is Overwork an Important Issue," *Sloan Work and Family Research Network*, 2005, http://wfnetwork.bc.edu/pdfs/EWS_Overwork.pdf (3 April 2006).

6. Lottye Bailyn, *Breaking the Mold: Women, Men, and Time in the New Corporate World* (New York: Free Press, 1993).

7. See Suzan Lewis and Jackie Dyer, "Towards a Culture for Work-Life Integration?," in *The New World of Work: Challenges and Opportunities*, ed. Cary L. Cooper and Ronald J. Burke (Malden, MA: Blackwell Publishers, 2002), 302–16.

8. An excellent perspective is offered by David M. Noer, *Healing the Wounds: Overcoming the Trauma of Layoffs and Revitalizing Downsized Organizations* (New York: John Wiley & Sons, 1995).

9. Joanne Ciulla, *The Working Life*, 161–62.

10. Richard Donkin, *Blood, Sweat and Tears: The Evolution of Work* (New York: Texere, 2001), 322.

11. Arlie Hochschild, *The Time Bind: When Work Becomes Home and Home Becomes Work* (New York: Metropolitan Books, 1997). Also see Arlie Hochschild, "When Work Becomes Home and Home Becomes Work," *California Management Review* 39, no. 4 (Summer, 1997): 79–97. Hochschild, drawing from a pioneering field study of an anonymous Fortune 500 company, has noted that "the longest hours at work were logged by the most educated professionals and managers." She further asserts that "one reason some workers feel more 'at home' at work is that they feel more appreciated and more competent there."

12. Robert Reich, *The Future of Success* (New York: Knoff, 2000), 5.

13. Thomas Merton, *Seeds* (Boston: Shambhala, 2002), 4.

14. Galinsky, Kim, and Bond, *Feeling Overworked.*

15. Reported in Barbara Reinhold, "An Uneasy Truce: Life/Work Balance for Executives," http://executive.monster.com/articles/balance/ (10 September 2001).

16. Reported in Sarah Roberts, "Survey Confirms that Americans are Overworked, Overspent, and Rethinking the American Dream," *The New American Dream 2005*, http://www.newdream.org/newsletter/survey.php (31 January 2005).

17. Jane Sturges and David Guest, "Working to Live or Living to Work? Work/Life Balance Early in the Career," *Human Resource Management Journal* 14, issue 4 (2004): 5–20.

18. Linda Duxbury, Christopher Higgins, and Donna Coghill, "Voices of Canada: Seeking Work-Life Balance," http://labour-travail.hrdc.qc.ca/worklife/welcome-en.cfm (29 July 2004).

19. "Actual and Preferred Working Hours," *Monthly Labor Review* 127, issue 6 (June, 2004): 77.

20. Jeffrey H. Greenhouse, Karen M. Collins, and Jason D. Shaw, "The Relation Between Work-Family Balance and Quality of Life," *Journal of Vocational Behavior* 63, no. 3 (2003): 510–31.

21. Reported in *Management Services* 48, issue 3 (March, 2004): 7. These findings are consistent with other research. For example, a Gallup study found that workers who adjusted their schedules to accommodate family concerns were less likely to get ahead. Therefore, employees with strong upward mobility potential were often unlikely to take advantage of family-friendly practices that existed in their respective organizations. For further detail, see Diane E. Lewis, "Firms Need to Support Work-Life Benefits," *Boston Globe,* 24 March 1998, C5.

22. For a more complete look at burnout, see C. Maslach, "Burnout: A Multidimensional Perspective," in *Professional Burnout: Recent Developments in Theory and Research,* ed. W. B. Schaufeli, C. Maslach, and T. Marek (New York: Taylor & Francis, 1993), 19–32.

23. The link between emotional intelligence (including themes such as optimism and resiliency) and one's career advancement has received solid backing. For example, see Steven J. Stein and Howard Book, *EQ Edge: Emtional Intelligence and Your Success* (New York: John Wiley & Sons, 2006).

24. Lou Tice is chairman of the Pacific Institute, an international organization that emphasizes leadership development and organizational change. These remarks were part of a 2004 presentation for a Fortune 500 company.

25. Rosamund Stone Zander and Benjamin Zander, *The Art of Possibility: Transforming Professional and Personal Life* (Boston, MA: Harvard Business School Press, 2000), 1.

26. An excellent review and perspective is offered by MacInnis and de Mello. Although their applications are marketing-oriented, the conceptual basis of hope is illuminating. Deborah J. MacInnis and Gustavo E. de Mello, "The Concept of Hope and Its Relevance to Product Evaluation and Choice," *Journal of Marketing* 69 (January, 2005): 1–14. Additional foundational work is provided by Richard S. Lazarus, "Hope:

An Emotion and Vital Coping Resource Against Despair," *Social Research* 66, no. 2 (1999): 653–60.

27. Diane Fassel, *Working Ourselves to Death: The High Cost of Addiction and the Rewards of Recovery* (New York: HarperCollins, 1990).

28. Work plays a key role in overall life satisfaction. In particular, research indicates a significant relationship between job satisfaction and life satisfaction. For example, see K. A. Loscocco and A. R. Rochelle, "Influences on the Quality of Work and Nonwork Life: Two Decades of Review," *Journal of Vocational Behavior* 39 (1991): 182–225; and M. Tait, M. Y. Padgett, and T. T. Baldwin, "Job and Life Satisfaction: A Reevaluation of the Strength of the Relationship and Gender Effects as a Function of the Date of the Study," *Journal of Applied Psychology* 74 (1989): 502–7.

29. Stewart D. Friedman and Jeffrey H. Greenhaus, *Work and Family—Allies or Enemies? What Happens When Business Professionals Confront Life Choices* (Oxford: Oxford University Press, 2000), 121.

30. In addition to Friedman and Greenhaus, this argument has been forwarded by others and has received considerable contemporary backing. For example, see Stewart D. Friedman, Perry Christensen, and Jessica DeGroot, "The End of the Zero-Sum Game," in *Harvard Business Review on Work and Life Balance* (Boston, MA: Harvard Business Review Paperback, 2000), 1–10; and Lotte Bailyn, Robert Drago, and Thomas A. Kochan, "Integrating Work and Family Life: A Holistic Approach," *A Report of the Sloan Work-Family Policy Network*, 2001; and Jeffrey H. Greenhaus and Gary N. Powell, "When Work and Family are Allies: A Theory of Work-family Enrichment," *Academy of Management Review* 31, no. 1 (2005), 79–92.

31. B. W. Eagle, E. W. Miles, and M. L. Icenogle, "Interrole Conflicts and Permeability of Work and Family Domains: Are There Gender Differences," *Journal of Vocational Behavior* 50 (1997): 168–84.

32. We will discuss these data and identify key cues (what we term "cues of vulnerability") later in the book. We are not suggesting that understanding limits, drawn from data, is unimportant. Rather, we are cautious not to categorize, stereotype, and restrict the individuality of the balancing process. Further, we fight the formulistic perspective that can arise from adhering to the data as absolute guides.

33. One should carefully note that although we have the ability (in most cases) to behave in ways counter to our preferences, such behavior moves us from our comfort zone and generally requires more focused energy than if we are behaving consistent with our preferences. Accordingly, these out-of-preference responses are seen as "de-energizing."

Chapter Three

Whose Dream You Runnin' Down

David and Susan offered a special challenge as we worked with a group of professional couples. Both bright and accomplished professionals, Susan's reserved demeanor was a perfect contrast for David's outgoing, engaging personality. During our first break of the day, Susan approached us with a heartfelt plea. "You've got to help David learn to slow down and enjoy life. He's wound so tight, he just can't relax." Susan went on to indicate that David was beginning to show stress-related signs including deteriorating physical health. As a concerned spouse, Susan was understandably worried about David and the life course he had chosen.

Later in the day, David initiated a conversation with us. His comments were sincere, yet almost desperate. Realizing that he was pushing himself too hard, he offered a revealing explanation. "I've got to keep driving on." David explained that he was the first person in his extended family to ever graduate from college. He was the first and only family member to work in a managerial capacity. David's rapid organizational assent and current position as vice president of a large, international company were sources of enormous pride within the family. He shared that he held somewhat of a "celebrity status" at large family gatherings.

From David's point of view, he was pinned down by mixed messages. He realized, at a personal level, the eventual destructive impact of his current lifestyle. Yet, he had to succeed and win for his family. He carried the banner of family achievement, a banner that could never be allowed to dip.

While the details may vary, David's story is everyone's story. The quest for balance is complicated by the barrage of mixed messages that we receive. The mixed message is this: "I love you and care about you and want you to do what makes you happy. I would be happy, though, if you would do or be or become this certain thing." Or, stated more generally, "You need to do what's best for you, but here is the socially rewarded (and therefore correct) set of options." Sometimes these messages are subtle; sometimes they are self-imposed; and sometimes they are clear and intentional. In any event, these messages are potentially dangerous and emotionally destructive. When balance becomes a contest with a goal of securing the mythical outcomes of unanimous approval from not-so-impartial others, a disappointing outcome will ultimately emerge. It is an outcome laden with frustration, confusion, unhappiness, discontent, and insignificance. In this chapter, we will discuss the most common of these messages and how they can affect our sense of balance.

THE IMAGE IMPOSED: THE ROLE OF SIGNIFICANT OTHERS

Part of our sense of who we are and who we must be is drawn from the images created and imposed on us by the significant others in our lives.[1] This is what David faced in our opening example. These significant others may be family, friends, or peers. These are people with whom we are close, people whose opinions are important to us, people who are capable of affecting us precisely because we care about pleasing them and gaining their valued approval. Accordingly, we have a tendency to link our expectations of ourselves to the expectations we feel are being cast by these significant others. While a common response, we may find ourselves living another's dream rather than our own. With paraphrasing apology to rocker Tom Petty, we often ask, "Whose dream you runnin' down?"

We worked with Bill, a brilliant physician in his late 30s. Graduating at the top of his medical school class, he had built a successful and lucrative practice. He had respect among his peers and all the external trapping of success. Yet, he admitted that he was not fully happy and fulfilled by his role as a physician. When we looked deeper, we saw that he pursued medicine, initially, because his family (and particularly his father) charted this course for him early in his life. Certainly, medicine capitalized on his gifts of intellect and his natural talents for grasping the complexities of human physiology. Yet he still told us that he didn't feel balanced. A closer look provided clues that he was struggling with suppressed gifts — gifts that his environment (one he created, mind you) did not allow or support him in expressing. In his case, one apparent suppressed gift was that of teaching others about health rather than decreeing treatment. He reported that when he had opportunities to teach, he felt more fulfilled and satisfied than he normally did. Describing his normal medical routine, he noted feeling exhausted in dealing with his severely ailing patients. In our language, he seemed drained and de-energized. We surmised that his somewhat depleted condition arose both from the extensive demands of a challenging patient population and from not fully utilizing his passion for shaping young medical minds.

It is important to note that Bill recognized his own struggle. So, you ask, why didn't he change? Bill provided the answer, indicating that he respected his father more than any person he'd ever known and stating that he would never want to do any thing to disappoint his father. What we have is a seasoned professional, torn by mixed messages.

Realize that in both David's and Bill's cases, their significant others never directly or knowingly attempted to deliver a mixed message. In fact, we surmise that if either had a sit-down, heart-to-heart talk with their family members, these loved ones would be overtly supportive of whatever would bring David and Bill contentment and happiness.

Indeed, partners and spouses are often able to bring their creativity and commitment to one another to bear to find the most ideal solutions, often discovering new options along the way. We are reminded of a woman we encountered at a workshop who told us the story of her husband, a successful patrolman with the local police department. For several years, he bounced from job to job; avoiding the quiet passion he had for law enforcement and public service by convincing himself that this was not a career for a man who wants to have a family. It wasn't until one night several years later, while on a late-night neighborhood walk that through his tears and angst, he communicated to his wife that this is what he wanted to pursue. She encouraged him to do so, and communicated that she did not, in fact, share his feelings that law enforcement was an unacceptable occupation. Even now, with a successful dual-career marriage, she wonders how she missed the mixed message he was experiencing, even if she was not sending it. "Sure, I get concerned about his welfare, now and then, but I've lived with him when he is unhappy, and I'd much rather live with him now!"

Importantly, all of these mixed message experiences are common. Most of us are not blindly rushing through life in pursuit of something that is counter to our core self. Rather, we are simply not fully expressing all that our core self embodies. We have suppressed gifts and dreams, and often they are suppressed because we use others' messages to guide decisions. We have said earlier that untapped or underutilized gifts are key pieces of an imbalanced life. In the same manner, suppressed gifts are often part of the foundation of imbalance.

At this point, it is important to realize that the concept of mixed messages as they apply to *your* livelihood and *your* sense of balance is a thorny one. Mixed messages often reside just beneath the surface of our consciousness and therefore may often go unrecognized. They affect us subtly as an emotional undercurrent. They act as invisible standards toward which we are always striving, yet we have no hand in creating. Importantly, they contribute to a sense of "not being good enough," which further undermines our well-being and our confidence in righting the situation.

Our work suggests that most people outwardly attend to the demands of these mixed messages only when forced to do so by the prompting of some strong emotional event. Our hope here is that you conduct a careful personal inventory to assess if you have been subjugating your sense of meaning to that inferred and crystallized from unrecognized mixed messages.

For a moment, we'd like you to reflect. Think about the messages you have received regarding your career and professional image. These messages may have come from family, respected authority figures (including teachers), friends and peers. They may even be drawn from media images that seem important and relevant. Who are you "supposed" to be? Now, is that consistent with who you are, who you want to be, who your gifts and purpose guide you to be?

Realistically, all of us live others' messages to some extent. We are social animals, and we do strive to please others, not in a pathological way, but in a way fundamental to human relationship and commitment to one another. Yet, when that attempt to please, even in the context of important relationships, begins to be diminishing rather than affirming, attention must be paid. You can provide that attention sooner or later. We opt for sooner.

You can probably identify with examples. You are successful. You are talented. Yet, you are imbalanced. Perhaps one reason why is your attention to mixed messages of valued others as a substitute for the messages coming from within. Often, though, we do not realize the gross amount of undue attention these messages are being paid—that is, not until we are faced with them in such a way that is impossible to ignore. For the would-be police officer, it was an emotional walk with his wife. For David, our reluctant physician, it was while coming to terms with dissatisfaction with a career that seemed nothing less than perfect. While these experiences provided the springboard to a different and more fulfilling career, it was not without paying the emotional price of allowing the unrecognized mixed messages to be too dominant for too long.

THE IMAGE ASSUMED:
THE ROLE OF COMPARISON OTHERS

Drawing from broadly accepted behavioral perspectives known as equity theory and social comparison theory, the role of comparison or referent others has been examined extensively.[2] Comparison others are people we feel are very much like us, people with whom we should logically be comparing ourselves. They may be colleagues or associates or they may be friends. They may even be families in the neighborhood that we do not really know but seem to be of similar age and social standing. Importantly, they are the people we select as relevant comparison others.

Make no mistake. We are a highly competitive lot, and these comparisons often provide us with images of our self-worth. Interestingly, studies show that we have a tendency to dramatically misperceive these comparison others. Typically, we feel that others are relatively better off than us, although objective evidence reveals that this is not the case.[3] In short, there is a tendency to overvalue the comparison other relative to us. Further, most comparisons with others take place without solid or actual comparison information.[4]

In part, our anguish with balance and imbalance is drawn from these comparison images that we assume or create. Often, we seem to gaze, quite superficially, on these images. We see others who seemingly have it all together. Their marriages are idyllic; their children are well behaved and truly gifted; their jobs produce high recognition and reward; and they are community stalwarts. We can almost hear Garrison Keiler in the background reveling in his Lake Woebegone comparisons where "all the men are strong, the women good looking, and the children above average."

Not surprisingly, the projected outer image of these comparison others becomes our barometer of self judgment and our gauge of personal satisfaction. And in a competitive, "tough as the other guy" social context, these comparisons can be powerful drivers of our behavior.

Thus, overly-glamorized "comparison others" push us to work more and drive harder. In the process, we inevitably fall short and experience dissatisfaction and disappointment. Of course, we only see the surface, not the emotion and not the inner spirit. We see nothing beyond others' carefully cultivated social masks. If we could strip away and glimpse others' private selves, we'd probably be both amazed and comforted that, in most cases, these idealized role models experience the same confusion and chaos that we do.[5] But, of course this is not the picture we see. There is a sort of sad solace in such realizations. Further, recognizing the true condition of these references could serve to release us from the stranglehold of unrealistic and inaccurate comparisons.

But, this is not what we do, at least in most cases. Our desire to have what they have intensifies our discontent and spurs us to make adjustments. Our perceptions of others and the assumed images they project create dissonance and move us to pursue the image. Again, we fall victim to mixed messages.

THE MYTH OF HAVING IT ALL

At the end of the day, significant others and comparison others help fuel the impression that we can have it all—successful careers, rich family lives, strong social networks, and ample time for physical, emotional, and spiritual health. With these comparisons firmly in mind, we believe that we should be able to work long hours, coach the little league team, be involved in the community, and still have quality time for concentrated family activity. It will blend together into a happy synergy that makes life full and worth living. The logical concepts of tradeoffs, opportunity costs, and opportunities lost become marginalized by hopeful dreams. In the process, any semblance that boundaries and parameters of choice must be the disciplines of personal action is pushed aside in favor of a romanticized idealism.

Importantly and rather sadly, the myth of having it all is perpetuated through a broader social context.[6] Media images flood our minds with unreasonable impressions and prescriptions. We are wowed by the political candidate, fit and energetic, knowledgeable about all the issues, sensitive to all range of plights and conditions, surrounded by a warm and loving family upon whom he undoubtedly showers hours of concentrated time and attention. This, we reason, is the norm, and it is what we *should be*. The popular press adds additional fuel. They tell us can that we can indeed be superwomen and supermen, as long as we follow a certain prescribed plan. Even as we observe these images of bloated exaggeration, we sense it's all too good to be true. Interestingly though, the images still play on our psyche and taint our perspective. Our lives are not the images projected, but they exist as images we wish were ours.[7] Again, we often choose to reject reality in favor of blind hope in an illusion.

I remember the advice received as a doctoral student over twenty years ago. The senior professor leading the seminar held our respect through his record of success, his penetrating insights, and his candid appraisals and challenges to the young minds he was directing. It would be little stretch to say his students literally hung on his every word. At one point, as we explored the tricky world of work-family interface, the question was posed: "Is it possible to have a highly successful academic career and a highly successful marriage and family?" In typical fashion, he held nothing back. He commented that he knew many colleagues who had wonderful, fulfilling marriages and had cobbled together respectable careers. Yet, he reflected that by most objective standards their career achievements were decidedly mediocre. He further suggested that of those who had amassed the kinds of first-rate careers to which we aspired had done so, in most cases, at dramatic cost to their marital and family situations. He concluded that one could achieve mediocrity and be content. But for those who choose a path of superiority, tradeoffs were inevitable.

Hearing the message of this sage, a few in our group, perhaps those most seasoned by life's experiences, had already decided that success was not all that it was cracked up to be. A couple of us (and I was one) accepted the professor's perspective as reasonable and sadly prophetic. However, the majority, perhaps the more idealistic among us, decided they would be the exceptions to the rule and they would indeed "have it all." And the mixed messages simply build and build.

HIDING

Before we begin this section—a bit more deeply psychological and philosophical section—let's briefly summarize the previous discussions. It seems that a large part of what makes us feel out of balance comes from comparing ourselves to others. On the outside, comparison others may seem as though they have this life balance thing figured out. So, not only are we bombarded with messages in the popular press that work-life balance is attainable, we interpret the lives of others to be in balance as well.

So what do we do with this information and these impressions? Most times, we put up a front of our own, particularly to coworkers, supervisors, and others with whom we regularly interact. The intent of the front is to suggest that we too have it all in balance. We believe it may signal weakness, poor planning, or questionable decision making to admit feeling or being imbalanced.

Projecting and then living this masked self has two unfortunate consequences. First, a great deal of energy goes into perpetuating the mask and therefore hiding who we really are. This is energy that could be used to create a better sense of balance in our lives. Secondly, hiding leads us to feel removed and disconnected from other people. Since social support can be an important means of achieving a sense of balance, our hiding serves to thwart or block this critical resource.[8] Once again, we are perpetuating stereotypes about balance as well as obstructing our own progress, this time by hiding our struggles and our quest for balance from those around us.

Most alarming, though, is that the person from whom we may be hiding most is our selves! We avoid admitting to ourselves that certain important personal needs are not being met by particular life situations. This produces underlying tension and anxiety that something is missing, and we tend to label this underlying tension as "imbalance."[9] We avoid seeing our situations clearly and we refrain from objectively acknowledging what is abundant, because by doing so we may also need to acknowledge what is lacking. This is a key point: by ignoring what is lacking, we cannot see what is present. Consequently, we become incapable of appreciating and celebrating what meaning and significance that we do possess and should enjoy. You see, by acknowledging what is *not*, we have both perspective and permission to enjoy what *is*. All of this positive and affirming abundance is potentially squandered by the mask of hiding. We risk not only blocked messages but missed redemption.

ORGANIZATIONS TO THE RESCUE

There is a final and powerful mixed message, a message that is rooted (perhaps) in good intention. It has to do with the way organizations have responded to the 21st century battle cry for better life balance, and it is manifested in a proliferation of organizationally-supported, work-life initiatives.[10]

Some of these initiatives, such as fitness programs and cheaper health-care options are clearly geared toward improving employee emotional and physical health and well-being, thereby saving organizations money and boosting productivity. However, the overwhelming majority of these initiatives have a different focus and a single primary emphasis—flexibility. Consider the range of popular possibilities. Alternative work schedules, telecommuting, flexible work schedules, child care options, extended leaves following birth or adoption, personal days, and even mini-sabbatical leaves all have the similar theme of offering employees greater flexibility.

Therein lays both the promise and the problem. Certainly, these initiatives have been organizational responses to help ameliorate the tension between work and other domains of life. But are we any better off? Have these initiatives reduced or have they actually fueled our sense of imbalance?

To answer this question, we need to take a broader social perspective. A number of critics have argued that corporate initiatives generally serve to build closer ties and obligations to the organizations offering the initiatives. Consider the views of Lewis and Dyer as they discuss the unique plight of knowledge workers:

"(Knowledge workers) have control over their own working hours, and can be flexible to fit in family or other demands, which is the goal of family-friendly policies. Yet paradoxically they are the most likely to be under pressure, to work long hours. They have autonomy to decide how to work, but this is associated with greater feelings of responsibility for getting work completed. In fact, among knowledge workers greater flexibility and autonomy are often associated with more conscientiousness and longer working hours. These longer working hours are then construed as a choice, and pressure is intensified."[11]

These authors further suggest that growing connectivity serves to blur the boundaries between work and non-work. Therefore, the knowledge worker is constantly linked to the workplace as the physical place of work becomes more and more a non-issue.[12]

In our own work, we have explored this issue of connectivity in some detail. Respondents have indicated that while organizational support for connectivity offered considerable flexibility, the unwritten pressure to remain linked to work was strong. A typical response was that of a young manager who noted that he would get home from work about six in the evening, have dinner with his family, and play time with his two young children. Yet, he revealed that when the children went to bed at 8:00, he would then work, often electronically linked to his organization, until 11:00 or even later. Large blocks of the weekend were also spent "doing work" from home. The ease of connectivity allowed him to avoid weekend trips to the office. While he appreciated the corporate support that made these arrangements possible, he recognized that the potential for and expectation of "homework" meant he was generally working 20 hours or more each week from his home. Even more telling was his belief that this expanded commitment to work was exactly what the organization expected and hoped would happen. Interestingly, the manager did not blame the organization for this outcome. He accepted responsibility, admitting that the connectivity options gave him the chance to "get ahead of his projects."

Let us be clear. The potential with connectivity lies in the amazing flexibility it provides—flexibility that was barely imagined a generation ago. Yet, connectivity creates for many of us a need to do more by giving us the means to do more. We recognize both sides of this argument. Greater flexibility can have a positive balance impact. However, the evidence suggests that for our audience of managers and professionals, flexibility and connectivity often translate into a condition of longer days and more work. (Note the self-imposed mixed message in this instance)! In the process, the potential for lower levels of life balance becomes more and more likely.[13]

There is an even more significant issue and a deeper mixed message taking place. Work has now permeated home. Historically, managers have never really been able to leave the emotional rigors of work behind them simply because they had left the office and returned home. Talented, upwardly mobile professionals have always done extra work away from the office to meet job demands and gain advantage over less aggressive peers. But there were boundaries. The home always had an escape and refuge quality. Today, the boundaries are fluid, increasing the negative spillover, particularly of work on family and personal life.

So, here are the key questions. Is this fluidity good or bad? Is it necessary to draw clear lines of demarcation between work and other domains of life? Probably not. After all, technology offers myriad advantages never before imagined. Is there really a reason to believe that availability of work options will eventuate into the reality of more work?

Well, perhaps yes. The fundamental danger lays in the insidious nature of extended work. Like kudzu on a hillside, work creeps in and slowly and almost imperceptibly begins to choke out all life but its own. We must reiterate that the organization is only partially to blame. By virtue of our achievement-oriented life styles and our near-insatiable desires for recognition and success, we avail ourselves of the opportunities to extend ourselves, accomplish more, and deliver a bigger corporate punch. Corporate initiatives have simply provided the means to do so.

From the point of view of life balance, here is the bottom-line fallacy of many organizationally-supported balance initiatives. Organizations are providing work-intensive, work-committed people with the means to extend their crippling patterns of work-dominated behavior. If these people could selectively back away from work demands, they probably would not have balance-related issues in the first place. Therefore, a proliferation of flexibility options appears to be a dangerous and ultimately problematic approach for easing the pressures of imbalance. Note the irony here. Programs put in place to maximize balance actually are the vehicles for a more imbalanced lifestyle. Mixed messages? Definitely.

The argument can be extended even more broadly. In her thought-provoking book, *The Working Life: The Promise and Betrayal of Modern Work*, Joanne Ciulla presents an additional perspective. She fears that as work-life initiatives grow, people may become more likely to turn to work to uncover the underlying meaning and purpose of their lives. She offers concern and argues, "Of all the institutions in society, why would we let one of the more precarious ones supply our social, spiritual, and psychological needs? It doesn't make sense to put such a large portion of our lives into the unsteady hands of employers."[14] By helping employees seek and find the right combination or balance in their lives, organizations offer an ever-expanding range of initiatives and options. Accordingly, she argues, workers become increasingly dependent on work. She notes how dangerous this can become in our current business era, replete with downsizing and lost loyalty, and she contends that rather than enhancing balance, we are acting to assure our ultimate vulnerability.

We have already conceded that life balance programs and initiatives are put in place to increase the likelihood of greater long-term organizational profitability. Further, in a competitive economic model, we have accepted the basic logic of such a stance. Programs are developed and funded to address personal and social concerns, remove barriers to performance (physical and emotional), and generate greater productivity. We can argue that the stability of a competitive market system demands such a perspective.

Yet, let's not miss the mixed message, the behind-the-scenes culprit working here. In many organizations, the implied message (and the real cultural signal) is to do more work, not less. Therefore, it is not unusual to find that many initiatives offer a promise that receives little reinforcement from the command structure of contemporary organizations. A number of studies have concluded that "workplace and/or societal cultures and expectations deter those most in need from even applying for such programs, and less-than-supportive supervisors undermine the benefits of specific programs."[15] Further, there are often wide variances between program availability and actual usage, with most studies indicating relatively low rates of use.[16]

Consider the common example of extended pregnancy leave, or family leave for fathers. Extending family leave is a wonderful life balance opportunity, but this option is a meaningless gesture as long as the signal that talented fast-trackers receive is that any extended breach in organizational attachment will result in debilitative career impact. And the research suggests that this is exactly what often takes place.[17]

We have worked with a high-profile company that has experienced double-digit growth for over ten years. Today, it is buoyed by new, lucrative markets and its future targets appear even loftier than those already attained. Respected for its quality, customer focus, and integrity, most outsiders considered employment as a plum management assignment. The company espouses a strong family-friendly culture. Not surprisingly, bright, young managers have flocked to the firm, spurred on by challenging assignments and commensurate rewards.

Yet, as we worked with a number of the organization's managers, a dark underbelly of the company became more and more apparent. While proud and dedicated, managers increasingly were feeling pinched by the escalating demands being placed upon them. As these work demands grew and family and personal time slipped, many managers began to question whether they could ever do enough and accomplish enough. They even, unflatteringly, referred to the corporate culture as "the pressure cooker."

Many young managers felt torn between challenging activity and opportunity for advancement on one hand and disillusionment and disappointment on the other. Some of the best and the brightest decided to take their talents elsewhere. In fact, managerial turnover became an issue and finding enough talent to support corporate growth became not only a major concern, but a limiting condition of future growth. Efforts to throw more money, new work-family initiatives, and enhanced compensation packages at the problem were partially successful at best. Despite its bold and progressive strategy, we sensed an impending crisis of leadership that could define and restrict the company's prospects over the next five years.

It appeared to us, as somewhat enlightened outside observers, that there was a major disconnect between what was being said and what was being done. Unfortunately, far from being an isolated example, we've described an all-too-familiar scenario. Leadership and organizational culture pioneer Edgar Schein expressed it best. He reminds us that leaders can talk any values they want, but culture resides in what values and behaviors people believe truly count and are ultimately reinforced by the organization. Accordingly, the espoused culture and the real culture may bear only limited resemblance to one another.[18]

There is an even more extreme position on these organizational actions to be considered. Paula Caproni argues that efforts to promote work-life balance may actually *undermine* ones' efforts to live productive and meaningful lives. In a bold and admittedly provocative stance, she notes that much of the current discourse (surrounding work-life balance) "is built on a language and logic that are based in traditional models of bureaucratic organizations, and thus the discourse is likely to perpetuate—and perhaps further entrench— many of the problems it promises to alleviate."[19] Part of the reframing she suggests is captured in personal choices. For example, she shares that "I gave up the notion that I should find passion in my work and instead looked to where I could make the greatest contribution for the most people and sought to keep passion in the home with my husband and children."[20]

BEYOND THE MIX

What all of this means is that no one and no institution will guide you through toward the sense of meaningful balance you seek. It is a decidedly personal decision. Each of us has responsibility for making it happen. We cannot defer this charge to any others.

In the end, we all must address our own mixed messages. We are caught— caught between the hype that encourages us to live full, whole, and rewarding lives . . . and the belief that unwavering corporate commitment (typically demonstrated through long hours of dedicated work) is the path to success. Accordingly, it is not unusual for managers and professionals to engage in a pattern of living that perpetuates the corporate person and diminishes the whole person. Why we allow this to occur has been the topic of both research and conjecture.

In part, the struggle lies in our desire for success and the complexity of defining what this means. We are struck by the words of Victor Frankl: "Don't aim at success—the more you aim at it and make it a target, the more you are going to miss it. For success, like happiness, cannot be pursued; it must ensue, and it only does so as the unintended side-effect of one's personal dedication to a cause greater than oneself or as the by-product of one's surrender to a person other than oneself. Happiness must happen, and the same holds for success: you have to let it happen by not caring about it."[21]

We are caught, caught between the images of our significant others, our comparison others, organizational expectations, and our personal sense of what truly offers value and meaning. We feel angry, frustrated, and disappointed that we are being manipulated. Yet we are hesitant, cautious to embrace our destiny for fear we may be revealed and have to live in line with that revelation. So we anguish but don't act. We experience pain without redemption. In the next chapter, we discuss the definitions of balance that may actually further entrench us in imbalance, but we also begin to consider a more expansive view.

ANOTHER LOOK BEFORE YOU LEAP

"As an independent mother of two young children, I have been a devoted employee and probably a workaholic. I am beginning to realize that I need more balance so I can meet my commitment to my family life. Yet, this does not seem to be truly acceptable in my workplace. Who should compromise?"

This is an honest and penetrating question, and it depicts the complicated nature of the mixed messages we often face. You imply that your work is important to you, probably from a necessity point of view (providing for your family) but also from a personal satisfaction point of view. You also realize that your family has needs that you must provide, undoubtedly an awareness that is becoming clearer as your children get a little older. Against this backdrop is the broad corporate landscape where the message seems to be (at least as you see it) that work dominance should trump family considerations. With all this in mind, you ask, "Who should compromise?"

Ideally, the answer is both you and the organization should compromise to find an appropriate middle ground where your talents are utilized to benefit the organization and your life is not overwhelmed and totally consumed by organizational pursuits. This process of "mutual accommodation" requires open communication, a willingness to modify established practices (from both sides), and a true appreciation of the need to have a full life as a source of personal meaning. We've seen this mutual accommodation approach succeed.

In order for it to work, there are two basic organizational pieces that have to be in place. Managers must value your talent enough that they are willing to think more broadly than they have in the past, and they must have a fundamental respect for the complexity of their people. If these assumptions and beliefs are not in place, the organization has little incentive to work with you on this.

This leads us to another answer that may be deeper than the ideal of mutual accommodation. Let's be totally straightforward. At times, we must make our own way and find alternatives to enact our own sense of meaning. That may mean that we take strong action to pursue what we know is significant and valued. In short, it is ultimately our responsibility to carve through the range of mixed messages and strike our own path. If the organizational leaders are unable or unwilling to work with you on this, then your tradeoffs must be evaluated. You must stay true to who you are, what is valued, and what is meaningful.

We encourage you to begin this process of reframing by working with and through your organization's managers. Begin with a positive frame of mind, assuming there are acceptable answers for all sides. But if this strategy yields nothing but dead ends, the responsibility for change is yours.

NOTES

1. Social identity theory is useful within this context. The theory contends that the social categories to which one feels attached provides a "definition of who one is in terms of defining characteristics of the category—a self-definition that is part of the self-concept." See, M. A. Hogg and D. J. Terry (eds), *Social Identity Process in Organizational Contexts* (Philadephia: Psychology Press, 2001), 3.

2. Adam's pioneering work in equity theory has been subjected to extensive review and elaboration. His original framework is presented in Stacy Adams, "Toward an Understanding of Inequity," *Journal of Abnormal and Social Psychology* 67 (1963): 422–36. Also see S. J. Adams and S. Freedman, "Equity Theory Revisited: Comments and Annotated Bibliography," in *Advances in Experimental Social Psychology*, ed. L. Berkowitz (New York: Academic Press, 1976), 43–90.

3. T. P. Summers and A. S. DeNisi, "In Search of Adams' Other: Reexamination of Referents Used in the Evaluation of Pay," *Human Relations* 43 (1990): 497–511.

4. George R. Goethals and William M. P. Klein, "Interpreting and Inventing Social Reality," in *Handbook of Social Comparison: Theory and Research*, ed. Jerry Suls and Ladd Wheeler (New York: Kluwer Academic/ Plenum Publishers, 2000), 23–44.

5. Again, we see that comparisons are frequently not based on real comparison data, as noted by Goethal and Klein, "Interpreting and Inventing Social Reality."

6. A challenging perspective is offered by Sylvia Ann Hewlett, "Executive Women and the Myth of Having It All," *Harvard Business Review* 80, no. 4 (April, 2002): 66–73.

7. The dissonance created between our self concepts and projected images can ravage us with disequilibrium and internal tension. One response can be (and often is) to attempt to live the image, thereby reducing the perceived dissonance. Such an approach follows the motivational logic of cognitive dissonance theory, originally proposed by Festinger. See Leon A. Festinger, *A Theory of Cognitive Dissonance* (Evanston, IL: Row, Peterson, 1957).

8. Building networks of support is a key theme for addressing work-life balance. This approach or remediation has been emphasized in the pivotal work of Friedman and Greenhaus. See Stewart D. Friedman and Jeffrey H. Greenhaus, *Work and Family—Allies or Enemies? What Happens When Business Professionals Confront Life Choices* (Oxford: Oxford University Press, 2000), 121.

9. We uncovered this "emotional tension" argument in our earlier work. See Charles R. Stoner, Jennifer Robin, and Lori Russell-Chapin, "On the Edge: Perceptions and Responses to Life Balance," *Business Horizons* 48 (2005): 237–46.

10. Alan L. Saltzstein, Yuan Ting, and Grace Hall Saltzstein, "Work-Family Balance and Job Satisfaction: The Impact of Family-Friendly Policies on Attitudes of Federal Government Employees," *Public Adminstration Review* 61, no. 4 (July/August, 2001): 337–46.

11. See Suzan Lewis and Jackie Dyer, "Towards a Culture for Work-Life Integration?," in *The New World of Work: Challenges and Opportunities*, ed. Cary L. Cooper and Ronald J. Burke (Malden, MA: Blackwell Publishers, 2002), 305.

12. Lewis and Dyer, "Towards a Culture for Work-Life Integration?"

13. The research here is still a bit unclear. Two themes seem likely. Connectivity, particularly for managers and professionals, provides greater flexibility (a balance-enhancing option). But it also provides the likelihood of spending more time on work-related activities (a potentially balance depleting outcome).

14. Joanne Ciulla, *The Working Life: The Promise and Betrayal of Modern Work* (New York: Times Books, 2002), 16–17.

15. Salzstein, Ting, and Salzstein, "Work-Family Balance and Job Satisfaction," 454.

16. A recent survey of human resource professionals revealed that 61% believed that employees were reluctant to take benefits, such as flextime and telecommuting, because it could negatively affect their careers. Reported in *Management Services* 48, no. 3 (March, 2004): 7.

17. For example, see Charles R. Stoner and Richard I. Hartman, "Family Responsibilities and Career Progress: The Good, The Bad, and The Ugly," *Business Horizons* 33, no. 3 (May-June, 1990): 7–14.

18. See Schein's classic work, Edgar H. Schein, *Organizational Culture and Leadership* (New York: John Wiley & Sons, 2004).

19. Paula J. Caproni, "Work/Life Balance: You Can't Get There from Here," *Journal of Applied Behavioral Science* 40, no. 2 (June, 2004): 209.

20. Caproni, "Work/Life Balance," 216.

21. Victor E. Frankl, *Man's Search for Meaning* (New York: Touchstone, 1984), 12.

Chapter Four

A Rock and a Hard Place

Bright, articulate, and seemingly self-assured, Deb was a 31-year old finan-cial analyst for a large service organization. As we asked her what balance meant to her, she paused reflectively before responding. "Balance to me is feeling like you have a good mix. I don't think there's any ratio, and I think it changes for me all the time. There are some weeks where work is really de-manding and you have to put more focus on that. Maybe things at home take a lower priority. There are times there's something more urgent at home and maybe that goes up a little and work falls down in my priority a little bit. I think it changes all the time. For me, its just feeling like everything is as it should be or I am able to focus my attention where I need to.

Imbalance is feeling like you don't have control over the direction that things are going. Not that you are always going to have control over every-thing, but feeling like there are aspects that you are not directly able to affect. It's kind of like the weather. No matter what you do, no matter how you try to plan or arrange and shuffle things, nothing you do can affect that. And that to me is just kind of a feeling. I don't quite have a grasp on things."

One of the struggles in addressing life balance is the clumsy nature of the term itself. Some writers make little or no pretense at offering a definition at all. Others offer definitions so obtuse that they are of limited practical value. Executives, managers, professionals (and yes, even consultants and academ-ics) find themselves at a loss when trying to describe or present a coherent view of balance.

Consequently, it is frustrating (but not overly surprising) that some of our more commonly accepted views of balance are not only confusing and mis-leading but operationally impossible, serving, for the most part, to bind people with unnecessary guilt and anxiety. Further, these views offer no reasonable sense of direction or hope. In short, we are being bombarded by conceptions of balance that do little to enlighten and much to deflate our fragile search for a meaningful life.

In order to gain the most from this book, we encourage you to abandon or at least temporarily set aside whatever views or conceptions of balance you may already hold. Part of the journey of finding balance is to reframe what balance should mean in our lives.

However, before reframing, moving forward, and providing our expansive perspective of balance, it will be helpful to shine a light upon the narrow crevice in which you have been attempting to squeeze yourself. If you have felt ravaged by your own balance attempts, you have probably been striving not only to run down another's dream (as we discussed in the previous chapter), but to align yourself with a finite set of options for creating balance and therefore meaning. You arrive here having experienced the discomfort that comes when we find ourselves between a rock and a hard place. Although we want you to step out of this place as quickly as possible, we also want you to have a clear understanding of where you have been, so you are less likely to find yourself there again.

PURSUING A MIRAGE

Traditional conceptions of balance are misleading for three fundamental reasons. First, they view balance as an equity issue and thereby prescribe equality in the time and effort placed in various life roles, regardless of the individual's gifts and purpose. Second, they forward the notion that balance is an end state, a goal to be obtained, rather than a constant process of shifting who we are to be more in line with who we wish to become. Third, they view balance as a time issue rather than a meaning issue. Let's look carefully at each of these conceptions of balance.

AN EQUITY ARGUMENT

Jon, a rising corporate star for a large, global company, raised a familiar concern. Pressed by an expanding travel schedule and guilt-ridden for neglecting his wife and children (ages 10, 12, and 15), Jon searched for an answer to his harried and increasingly complicated life. Simplistically, he argued that time was the issue. While unwilling to back off his corporate commitments (and risk fast-track derailment), he looked for ways to gain more equitable blocks of time for his wife and kids. To him, balance would be achieved when he arranged all the pieces so everyone was satisfied and content. Predictably, he felt caught between a rock and a hard place.

His view of balance was framed by traditional balance thinking. Here, balance is projected as a carefully finessed synchronicity and lives are balanced when relatively equal parts of time, attention, and energy are assigned to the various realms of life. As noted in chapter one this view projects balance as a grand juggling assignment, where one courageously strives to keep all the pieces in play and given proper attention. Don't miss the underlying message here. This standard of balance suggests that all the pieces should be given full and needed attention. As such, people are prodded to valiantly attempt to structure not only a balanced life, but a perfectly balanced life. As if the standard were not high enough, our views of perfect balance are further bloated by the societal, familial, and personal ideals that we addressed in the previous chapter.

Even more damning, Jon was convinced that he could make it happen. He shared his conviction that to mishandle this juggling challenge would be a personal failure. He derisively concluded that he could not be seen as one of those guys who "can't deal with what he has on his plate."

There is a further, insidious depth to this argument. The reasoning suggests that not only do we invest ourselves in multiple dimensions of life, but we do so with equal time, energy, attention, and commitment. Popular and academically reputable sources perpetuate this view. Some studies, by way of example, have characterized work-family balance as "the extent to which an individual is equally engaged in—and equally satisfied with—his or her work role and family role."[1] These authors assert that "an individual who gives substantially more precedence to one role than another is relatively imbalanced even if the distribution of commitment to family and work is highly consistent with what the individual wants or values."[2] Accordingly, a balanced life is envisioned as "achieving satisfying experiences in all life domains," which of course requires that "energy, time, and commitment (are) well distributed across domains."[3] So here is the rock and the hard place. Satisfying experiences do not often come with equal time spent in each role. Yet, many definitions suggest that this is exactly what produces satisfying balance experiences. It is no wonder people feel stuck and see little hope of creating a life in balance.

THE PROBLEM-SOLUTION ARGUMENT

The second aspect of these types of definitions that is troublesome is their implication that there is a *solution* to the balance *problem*. Recognizing that balance generally is thrown into question when our various roles or identities (say work and family) begin to chip away at one another, one could argue that balance exists when stress is eliminated between work and family (or other key) roles.[4] We cannot champion this view of balance. Although the exploration of roles and role conflict are valuable dimensions in unraveling the balance picture, the elimination of stress seems impractical, unlikely, and even unproductive to us. We reject the stress-free notion of balance.

Other writers have viewed balance as "satisfaction and good functioning at work and home, with a minimum of role conflict."[5] While this step seems more reasonable because it is less restrictive, the definition still suggests a utopian "got it" that grinds against the edges of real living.

In short, we disagree that balance is a problem to be solved. Rather, we position balance as an ever-evolving need. Likewise, we chafe at the notion that there is some formulaic solution to our life balance search. Socially and personally, many of us have been damaged by the images and expectations that lead to the pursuit of some nebulous and elusive "ideal" balance. This pursuit can only take us to one place—a personal sense of diminishment and failure for having not accomplished the "goal" of balance implicit in the images and expectations. We've observed an additional consequence. Over time, otherwise successful and accomplished professionals tend to become paralyzed as their repeated attempts to achieve some prescribed utopia fall short.

This is known as "learned helplessness," a condition that has been well-researched and accepted.[6] Learned helplessness arises in situations in which an individual attempts to influence his or her environment and is unable to alter the status quo. As a result, influence activities cease. In essence, one is learning to be helpless. In the case of balance, we attempt to create feelings of satisfaction and "good functioning" over and over again, only to be met with the same feelings of incompleteness. Eventually, we cease our attempts to create balance, and instead resign ourselves to a life that is less than what we hoped it would be. Realize that such a response is natural and understandable. One mechanism by which our behavior is governed is by reinforcement. We tend to repeat what is rewarded and cease what is not. In this case, action is not rewarded. We are paralyzed between the rock and a hard place.

The gripping effect of the problem-solution view has been apparent in the lives of the professionals with whom we have worked. Consider the story of Rich, a 34-year old manager for a large service company. Rich was a hard-working professional whose ethic of dedication and results had catapulted him into a leadership position that was unusual for his level of formal education (high school diploma and various training and development programs). Rich's work performance was outstanding and he found his work satisfying. His responsibilities were challenging and engaging, his colleagues and direct reports were respected friends, and the rewards he earned were highly competitive. He and his wife spent their occasional leisure time traveling or working on their recently-purchased home.

There was uneasiness as we met with Rich. Over the next few minutes, Rich recounted how much enjoyed his job, even though 11-hour days and regular travel were part of his work regimen. His concern was that he was so focused on work that he was slighting his wife. As we probed, we were impressed with Rich's efforts to attend to the family dimension of life. He looked for activities he and his wife could do together on the weekends. He had implemented and carried through on a date-night for dinner during the week, and he included his wife in long-weekend travel as often as he could. Yet, he admitted that his job took the bulk of his time and that he felt emotionally torn that he did not give his wife either the time or energy he gave to his work. While their marriage was not unhappy, Rich sensed that the family dimension of his life was falling short of his personal expectations. Further, he reasoned that the way to more family satisfaction had to be to spend more time in family pursuits. Interestingly, when we asked, he was unable to define what additional activities he would pursue and instead offered a vague argument that "there just had to be more."

Rich's expectations of the work-family relationships were drawn from a number of mixed and socially questionable messages as discussed earlier. His condition was further exacerbated as Rich bought into the notion that greater equity in time between work and family would be the answer. Unfortunately, Rich's conception of balance and his pursuit of an unrealistic and unattainable ideal will always leave him with that "pit of the stomach" feeling that he is not quite doing enough. Additionally, Rich's response leads us to a third way individuals are mislead; they are led to believe balance is a function of time.

THE TIME ARGUMENT

The time argument is perpetuated because it has a certain intuitive appeal.[7] If we simply had more time, we'd be able to attend to all the competing demands that strain our efforts and restrict our potential for securing balance. The solution (given that we are unable to add hours to the day) is to find time saving techniques that allow us to etch out valued slots of time that were previously either wasted or handled poorly.

The time argument is rooted in a conflict model of work-life balance. Here, it is assumed that time spent participating in one role (say, work), confounds and may even restrict or eliminate participation in different roles (say, family). This scarcity view leads to depletive thinking—since time is a scarce and limited resource, attention focused in one area of life depletes the attention possible for other areas.[8]

Make no mistake. We certainly are advocates of good time management. Time management techniques can enhance efficiency, affect one's sense of accomplishment, and improve overall performance. However, we seriously question whether time management techniques will produce the perception of balance most people seek.

Our reasoning is drawn from our fundamental belief that balance is only partially a time issue. Let's consider an argument that we have presented in many of our workshops. Assume that you had two extra hours a day at your discretion. Would the extra time yield a better or fuller sense of balance? Although many of our workshop participants seem visibly relieved as they nod their heads with satisfaction at the prospect, we doubt it.

We have had been able to follow managers and professionals who have participated in and completed our Executive MBA program. The intensive 15-month program requires about 15—20 hours a week of extra time from individuals who are already swamped. Somehow, they find the time to meet the demands of the program. As each participant draws toward the end of their program, we have asked, "How will you use the extra 15 hours a week that you will now have available to you?" Understandably, part of the new-found "extra" time is committed to catch-up on projects that have been put on hold. But what of the rest? Most participants are elated just thinking about the ways their lives will change; how the pace will slow down; and how balance can be resurrected. Yet, as we meet with participants, only months after the program has ended, we find that their lofty hopes have not been realized. Soon, they are taking on extra projects at work, committing to more community volunteer work, and pushing harder on their selected career paths. Although there is nothing wrong with any of these endeavors, they do represent "more of the same." Often, participants tell us they feel less, not more, balanced as a result of the additional time they've acquired.

Here is another parallel. In the early days of human resource training, academics and practitioners alike evaluated the relative merits of job enlargement versus job enrichment as ways to promote individual motivation and satisfaction. Job enlargement involved giving people more things to do on the job. Job enrichment centered on giving people more meaningful things to do on the job. Not surprisingly, most people prefer the latter to the former. A similar logic applies to the balance topic. Simply giving people more time permits them to do more things, and often these are the same types of things they are already doing. Unless new activities extend or activate additional threads of meaning, it's unlikely that one's sense of balance will be positively affected.

The view that balance is a time issue and that we need more time in order to craft a balanced life is further ingrained through organizational patterns and messages. Indeed, the majority of corporate responses to life balance concerns are based upon structuring time (e.g., flextime, compressed work weeks, concierge services, and a growing range of leave and time-away-from-work initiatives). While well-intentioned, progressive, and appreciated, these initiatives will never fully capture the problematic nature of life balance because time is simply not the fundamental issue.

Having discussed the three misleading perspectives of balance: balance as a matter of equity, balance as a problem to be solved, and balance as a time issue. Let's move forward and consider some conceptions of balance that are more realistic, accurate, and consistent with life demands.

The perspectives we offer are attainable, which seems to be a reasonable prerequisite of any pursuit one would choose. In fact, the issue of realism is more important than most people realize. We venture to guess that you have a strong need for achievement. It is one reason you have attained the success you have. One characteristic of achievement-oriented people is the need to reach for challenging, but clearly realistic goals. An additional characteristic is an increased sensitivity to and frustration with wholehearted efforts that are not met with unmitigated success. As a first step, then, it is important to pursue a reality, not some far-off mirage that continually fails to materialize the harder we try to reach it. The views we discuss next represent one such reality. Of course, these views are also more congruent with the foundational themes of our work.

TAKING AN INTEGRATIVE VIEW OF BALANCE

The arguments we have just reviewed fall short in another critical regard. They encourage independent, segmented thinking about the various dimensions of a balanced life. As such, the obvious realization that various areas of life can overlap and affect one another is not given appropriate consideration. In reality, life tends to be rather fluid, eschewing the segmented distinctions that offer ease of theoretic modeling, but fail to capture the complexity of behavioral dynamics.

Responding to this criticism, an integrative view of balance, also known as the spillover hypothesis, is one of the more progressive research views of the past few years, and it has reframed our thinking about balance, particularly the balance between work and life. For example, this view argues that we should no longer view the tugs between career and family as "tradeoffs" between competing demands. As one group of authors argues, work versus personal life does not have to be a zero-sum game. Instead, "work and personal life are not competing priorities but complementary ones."[9] Others have even argued that most traditional images of balance are outmoded and should be replaced by a focus on integrating work and family time.[10] This theme of integration is fascinating and offers an important glimpse into the complex world of life balance.

In chapter two, we introduced the work of Friedman and Greenhaus, who argued that positive and helpful spillover (as well as negative and harmful spillover) was possible. Recognizing that work-family conflict is present when "one role detracts from the quality of life within the other role," the authors note that work-family integration occurs when "participation in one role enhances the quality of life in the other role."[11]

Recall that Friedman and Greenhaus emphasized emotional gratification, the satisfaction we experience when either work or family fulfills important goals and needs. Recognizing that "the level of emotional gratification we experience in one domain directly affects our level of emotional gratification in the other," the authors posit that this resulting emotional "spillover" can lead to positive outcomes of integration or negative outcomes of conflict.[12]

Let's consider an example. Most of us have had the experience of working a long, challenging but successful day. Outcomes were achieved and our unique skills were tapped and utilized. We feel good. While it is true that our energies have been depleted, it is also true that we are excited and buoyed by our work experiences. These positive emotions carry over as we greet our families and engage our friends. Likewise, affirming and supportive interactions at home and in the community give us the upbeat outlook and "can do" attitude that make us successful at work. Further, encouraging the integration of the work-family-community-social realms can produce synergies such as the above with little or no additional time expended. This further supports our point that balance is not a time issue.

Of course, negative spillover is also likely. But, if we focus here, striving for the elimination of negative spillover, we are back to creating segmented lives where work time and family time (as well as other life dimensions) are compartmentalized and treated as independent entities rather than pieces of a "whole" life. As if the stress of constantly maintaining this unnatural boundary between life roles were not enough, we also diminish positive spillover by rigidly adhering to conceptions of "work time" or "family time". In actuality, negative spillover is a cost of living a whole life, but the price is fair if one is also cultivating positive spillover. Here's the point. If we segment to avoid negative spillover, by definition we obscure the power and significance of positive spillover. One can't have it both ways. This theme is further described in the second half of the book.

Let's review the relationship of the spillover hypothesis and our fundamental perspectives on balance. We suggest that heavy involvement in any given dimension of life does not necessarily detract from another dimension. In fact, it can synergistically improve it and enhance one's overall sense of life balance.

We have discussed how individuals may be misled by well-intentioned, but restrictive definitions of balance. And, we have contended that work, life, and other roles are integrative rather than isolated and independent. It seems, to this point, we have discussed much more about what balance is not than what balance actually is. Many of the executives and professionals we interviewed in our work could not define it in the affirmative sense; rather, they described what balance was not, much as we have above. Make no mistake, balance is not easily defined. In order to move forward, though, we need to firmly and succinctly zero in on the elusive balance. With this in mind, it is time to turn to our conception of life balance. It is time to reframe.

SEARCHING FOR A BETTER WAY

Joan Kofodimos' pioneering work, *Balancing* Act, gets close to a workable definition of balance. Kofodimos asserts that the term balance deals with "a satisfying, healthy, and productive life that includes work, play, and love; that integrates a range of life activities with attention to self and to personal and spiritual development; and that expresses a person's unique wishes, interests, and values. It contrasts with the imbalance of a life dominated by work, focused on satisfying external requirements at the expense of inner development, and in conflict with one's true desires."[13] While she does not use the word "meaning", she clearly is embracing some of the same themes we have advanced as foundations of our work for creating a balanced life. Moreover, her definition acknowledges the range of life experiences, roles, and activities that individuals in a state of balance possess. She does not draw distinctions between life roles, which is another key aspect of our own thinking about balance.

Other researchers take this notion even further. Chalofsky notes that "the sense of balance at its ideal is that life is so integrated that it does not matter what one is doing so long as it is meaningful."[14] We agree with Chalofsky's intent and practicality. Yet, we still struggled with the question, "what is an integrated life?" We acknowledge that this concept may offer as much confusion as it offers hope. However, consider the final phrase of his definition: "it does not matter what one is doing so long as it is meaningful." This sense is important and wraps the idea that balance is all about finding "personal meaning."

The Point

In reality, our perspective or definition of balance has nothing to do with the historical and conventional assumptions that have led to the use of the term "balance" in the first place. We use the term only to provide consistency with the popular label most have given to what they seek in reading a book such as ours. In our view, balance is the experience of meaning that arises when one's gifts and purpose are aligned with one's life situation. Said another way, it is the ongoing, personal awareness that one's life *is* meaningful when it is lived in pursuit of a higher purpose and supported by the application of one's unique gifts and values. Stated in terms of behavior, the more actions one takes throughout the day in pursuit of this purpose, while using their gifts and values, the more one experiences meaning and therefore balance.

Stop right there! Lest your compulsion is to slam this book shut, throw it on the end table, and reach for your Franklin planner as a means to avoid the esoteric diatribe that you assume will come next, let us clarify and expand our thinking by bringing you back to the world of work. The definition we provided is, in fact, general. But a good definition is both general and practical.

Above all, balance is a personal perception or impression. Many of the people we have worked with have all the pieces necessary for a balanced life, but are drawn away from a sense of contentment and meaning by the harsh images, unrealistic expectations, and weighty demands they receive from external sources. As such, their personal sense of balance is skewed and their contentment thwarted. Others, however, march to their own beat with surprising outcomes.

For example, we worked with Leia, a successful middle-aged leader and activist whose life, from all external observations, is a hectic hodge-podge of activity. An encounter with Leia is a blur of motion, as she bounces from idea to idea, at times focusing intently and at times anxious to disengage. Yet Leia is incredibly balanced. Leia's gifts are her creativity, her energy, and her penetrating insight into people coupled with a genuine concern for others' well-being. Her purpose (or more appropriately purposes) are heady and ever-evolving. Yet they include a strong commitment to helping others reach their personal potential as they navigate the complexities of life. Her work as a high school counselor, her volunteer activities through her church, and her loving relationship with her family each allow her to manifest her gifts and purpose in amazing and powerful ways. Her life is full and not without stress. However, she experiences meaning and according to our definition, life balance.

Or consider the case of Shay. We first met him when he attended a multi-week leadership series we conducted. In his mid-40s, Shay had secured a series of promotions during his twenty year career that were designed to broaden his experience and groom him for upper-level management. Bright and articulate, he had achieved the director level in a large international business. While he was not passionate about the content of his current job duties, he was committed to his organization and to his own personal growth and development. He sensed that something was missing, which was the primary reason he established an in-depth coaching relationship with us. Realize that from all external trappings, Shay epitomized success and balance. While Shay was not dissatisfied, he longed for something more.

As we talked to Shay about his work, he beamed with excitement when discussing the weekly meetings he held with young, high potential associates in the company, a task he assumed not only for his direct reports but for a range of associates who others referred to him. It seemed that Shay had gained a reputation among young professionals in the organization for being a supportive and knowledgeable mentor. Without realizing it, Shay had found an outlet for his gifts and purpose that fell outside the boundaries of his current job description. In Shay's case, his job did not necessarily provide meaning, but it did provide the context in which Shay discovered meaning for himself.

With this background, we encouraged Shay to look for ways his gifts might be utilized more fully. His first response was to outline several areas in which he had already taken on an advisory or mentoring role. For example, he coached his son's soccer team and served on the local park district board. We pushed Shay and asked how he could make his obvious talents at coaching young professionals a more pronounced part of his professional life. You see, work is very important to Shay. It is a large part of his life. In order to truly experience meaning, Shay could not relegate his gifts merely to off-hours expression. Consequently, Shay volunteered for internal mentoring assignments and even taught at a local university. This brought him closer to contentment, which only whetted his appetite for further meaning.

Interestingly, today Shay finds himself a trailing spouse for the first time. The position he and the organization have agreed upon? He is directing a new project task force that identifies and creates development opportunities for young talent throughout the company. In this role, he works closely in leading the assessment and mentoring actions so near and dear to him. He has talked with us about the clear alignment of his gifts with his job duties. He speaks with energy and satisfaction. We call it balance!

Make no mistake, balance is hard won. Leia's and Shay's cases are not unique, but they did not arrive at their current states easily, nor will they be able to grow and continue to experience balance without vigilance, informed choices, and continual adjustments and recalibration.

Another theme is embedded here. We want to be sure that it is not lost in the detail of this chapter. Our definition of balance can be a freeing and empowering realization as much as it is a call for action. Many people are closer to the experience of balance than they realize or permit themselves to believe.

Let's look at the example of Catherine, a 28-year old fast-tracker in her organization. She came to our workshop believing that her life was undoubtedly out of balance. Focusing a disproportionate amount of time and energy on her career, she felt guilty for the time she was not spending with her husband. That guilt got in the way of enjoying the time she did spend with him, which upon probing, was not an unreasonable amount of time given their respective careers and life situations. Yet, she was convinced that her ten-hour workdays had to be modified. She looked to us for guidance.

We encouraged reflection and careful consideration of her gifts and purpose. Somewhat grudgingly, she acquiesced to some of our balance exercises (which we discuss later in the appendix of the book). Almost as a revelation, Catherine came to realize that her work made her who she was—alive, creative, engaged, and impassioned. The confidence she experienced in her career allowed her to manifest her strengths in other areas, including her church and community. It was precisely through her work and the meaning she derived from work that she became the inspired and inspiring woman her husband adored. After the session, Catherine's comments showed she realized a fresh perspective toward balance that was truly liberating. No longer was she burdened by a heavy sense of guilt. Rather, she enthusiastically commented, "I'm happy with my life and where I am headed. I really am balanced after all." This reframe was no simple mind game or minor perceptual shift; rather, she understood in a powerfully personal way that the engagement of her gifts and movement toward a meaningful and evolving purpose provided what she wanted and needed from life.

If there is one thing we know for sure, it is that mature, well-adjusted people do *not* grow from an ideal or vision that is limiting or restrictive. Attempting to craft meaning, using personal gifts and individualized life purpose, simply does not happen within the confines of a cookie-cutter definition of work-life balance. When attempting to do so, important gifts that fall outside the boundaries established by the definition go unused. Moreover, personal qualities and characteristics that are not, in fact, true gifts, are nurtured in vain and the professional is left feeling inadequate and incompetent. Families, work groups and communities suffer when people attempt to fit themselves into this mold. As eloquently put by Harold Whitman, "Don't ask yourself what the world needs. Ask what makes you come alive. Because what the world needs are people who have come alive."[15]

Accordingly, people *do* grow when given fertile ground—affirmation of gifts and purpose and the potential these hold, permission to dream of possibilities, and support through the personal journey of discovery. If balance really is: "the experience of meaning that arises when one's gifts and purpose are aligned with one's life situation," a whole new world opens to us. Much of the second half of the book is devoted to making this definition as practical as possible without allowing it to become yet one more cookie cutter. In short, we provide the fertile ground needed to grow. We are inspired by the words of Viktor Frankl: ". . . the true meaning of life is to be discovered in the world rather than within man and his own psyche as though it were a closed system."[16]

ANOTHER LOOK BEFORE YOU LEAP

"You've talked a lot about work-life integration, and you've said this term is probably a better description of the true path to meaning. But, I really don't want to integrate my life. Work stays at work. Home stays at home. It is unfair to bring either into the other. It would also compromise my sanity to do so."

We often answer this question by reminding our participants that there is a semantic issue at play here, but we also must acknowledge the very real fear inherent in this question as well. First, the question is based on the time-honored conception that one is happier and better balanced by making clean demarcations between work, home, and other areas of life. It's a bold and inspiring proposition. The trouble is, it doesn't make sense. It is a futile attempt to accomplish the impossible.

We see the concern. For example, calls and assignments from work may make time with a spouse half-hearted at best and non-existent at worst. Likewise, who can focus on a client presentation if he is concerned that his child is failing algebra? This is a classic example of fixed-pie mentality, which assumes that attention spent in one area cannot also support and fuel success in another. We submit to you that there is another way of thinking about integration.

Let's start with some personal reflection. Have you ever had an exciting, successful day in which you felt competent, in-charge, and valued at work? And, has that positive energy ever carried over into your evening? Were interactions with others better because of it? Every professional has probably had this experience. This is the type of integration we encourage you to examine and appreciate. By the same token, most of you have had experiences where non-work celebrations have lifted your spirits and prompted more creativity and goodwill toward co-workers.

And, then, the follow-up thinking comes. "You are too optimistic. What I am talking about is what happens when I have an awful day at work, or when my spouse and I have a fight just as I am stepping out the door."

Our response is realistic. Pretend as you might, you cannot separate them. Your work will be affected by the argument. Dinnertime will be more tense following an awful day. The energy you expend trying to cordon off emotions and concerns in one area of life from the others only adds to your levels of stress and frustration. We would be better off most of the time by admitting and accepting the spillover and working with it rather than against it. That does not mean we are paralyzed or incapacitated by that spillover. It also does not mean that we expose emotional vulnerability at inappropriate times or in inappropriate venues. Work still must be done. Goals must be accomplished. Family time must be full and personal. But there is value in the acknowledgment of spillover, whether that acknowledgment is to yourself or to others.

Again, let's turn to an example. We recently worked with a senior executive who clearly was distracted and mentally absent from our conversation. With only minor probing, he shared that his wife was experiencing serious health issues that logically were capturing his time and attention. Once he shared his concerns about his wife, two things happened. First, he was more readily able to discuss the items on our agenda. But secondly, any solutions or suggestions took this important life event into account. Since we now had a better understanding of his personal landscape, we were able to suggest some alternatives that were responsive to his life situation.

So, what does all of this mean? Spillover does affect you. Life cannot be segmented. And we are only fooling ourselves if we think otherwise.

NOTES

1. Jeffrey H. Greenhaus, Karen M. Collins, and Jason D. Shaw, "The Relation Between Work-Family Balance and Quality of Life," *Journal of Vocational Behavior* 63 (2003): 513.

2. Greenhaus, Collins, and Shaw, "The Relation Between Work-Family Balance and Quality of Life," 513.

3. Catherine Kirchmeyer, "Work-Life Initiatives: Greed or Benevolence Regarding Workers' Time," in *Trends in Organizational Behavior,* ed. C. L. Cooper and D. M. Rousseau, 7 (West Sussex, UK: Wiley, 2000), 81.

4. See commentary provided by Haron Alisha Lobel, "Allocation of Investment in Work and Family Roles: Alternative Theories and Implications for Research," *Academy of Management Review* 16, no. 3 (1991): 507–21.

5. Sue Campbell Clark, "Work/Family Border Theory: A New Theory of Work/Family Balance." *Human Relations* 53, no. 6 (2000): 751.

6. C. Peterson, S. F. Maier, and M. E. P. Seligman, *Learned Helplessness: A Theory for the Age of Personal Control* (New York: Oxford University Press, 1993). Martin Seligman has done pioneering work in the arena of both learned optimism and learned helplessness. See Martin Seligman, *Learned Optimism* (New York: Pocket Books, 1991).

7. Lottye Bailyn has noted, "time is the most critical issue in the ability to integrate one's private and public lives." Lottye Bailyn, *Breaking the Mold: Women, Men, and Time in the New Corporate World* (New York: Free Press, 1993), 79.

8. This line of thinking is logical and has deep conceptual roots. See, for example, the views of the Nobel laureate economist Gary Becker. Gary S. Becker, "Human Capital, Effort, and the Sexual Division of Labor," *Journal of Labor Economics* 3, no. 1 (1985): 35–58. Also see J. H. Greenhaus and N. J. Buetell, "Sources of Conflict Between Work and Family Roles," *Journal of Management Review* 10 (1985):76–88.

9. Stewart D. Friedman, Perry Christensen, and Jessica DeGroot, "The End of the Zero-Sum Game," in *Harvard Business Review on Work and Life Balance* (Boston, MA: Harvard Business Review Paperback, 2000), 3.

10. Rhona Rapoport, Lottye Bailyn, Joyce K. Fletcher, and Bettye H. Pruitt, *Beyond Work-Family Balance: Advancing Gender Equity and Workplace Performance* (San Francisco: Jossey-Bass, 2002).

11. Stewart D. Friedman and Jeffrey H. Greenhaus, *Work and Family—Allies or Enemies? What Happens When Business Professionals Confront Life Choices* (Oxford: Oxford University Press, 2000), 122.

12. Friedman and Greenhaus, *Work and Family—Allies or Enemies? What Happens When Business Professionals Confront Life Choices*, 127.

13. Joan Kofodimos, *Balancing Act: How Managers Can Integrate Successful Careers and Fulfilling Personal Lives* (San Francisco: Jossey-Bass, 1993), xiii.

14. Neal Chalofsky, "An Emerging Construct for Meaningful Work," *Human Resource Development International*, 6, no. 1 (2003): 79.

15. Quoted in Donna Karlin, "Perspectives: Insights of an Executive Shadow Coach" http://betterperspectives.blogspot.com/2005/06/dont-ask-yourself-what-world-needs.html (10 April 2006).

16. Victor E. Frankl, *Man's Search for Meaning* (New York: Touchstone, 1984), 133.

Part Two

Chapter Five

The Elephant in the Room

Anna is a successful hospital administrator, a single mother, and a new home-owner. She is incredibly active by nature, and her positive attitude is infectious. She is also very practical, striving for efficiencies in the use of both her time and her finances. Having just moved to a new city, she renewed her commitment to "doing it all." She dove into remodeling projects immediately after unpacking, and soon (on top of her career and parenting responsibilities), she established a social network and a group of close friends. Each weekend was a whirlwind of activity, one that often began on Friday when Anna would vow to use her time to finish paperwork and the week's reports, spend quality time with her young daughter, run errands and complete the grocery shopping, move forward on the bathroom tiling project, and nurture her newfound friendships. While truly optimistic, practical, and efficient, Anna found herself feeling incompetent, inefficient, and exhausted each Sunday evening. One spring day she called to say, "I just figured it out. For the last year, I have been dismissing my feelings of incompetence as illogical instead of paying attention to what they had to tell me. Once I did, I learned that I have been trying to do way too much on the weekends. You'd be proud of me. I finally hired a housekeeper and a lawn service!" Of course, Anna had just discovered what many of us had always known, simply by paying attention to her feelings, thoughts, and behaviors rather than missing or dismissing this crucial data. Once she began to attend to what was happening internally, she was able to take action to bring her life into better balance.

In the previous chapter, we presented traditional conceptions of balance, explored some key shortcomings of these views, and detailed our perspective on balance. Our contention that balance centers on meaning justly underscores the idiosyncratic and personal nature of the topic. In this chapter, we launch you on your own quest for balance in a way that may at first seem counterintuitive, by focusing upon imbalance.

It is apparent from our research that, for most people, balance is not really something that is regularly contemplated. As one respondent told us, "Balance isn't something you think about when you're running at 120 miles an hour." On the other hand, most of us are compelled to pay attention when confronted with the harsh impacts of imbalance.

Consider a simple analogy. One does not normally think much about the life-sustaining significance of the air we breathe; that is, until that air becomes tainted or compromised or limited in some way. As one breathes and is confronted by the unexpected gasp of insufficiency, signals of alarm spark through the body at both physiological and psychological levels. We are consumed by efforts to restore or replenish our necessary supply of acceptable air. Perhaps it is mere understatement to note that the perceived deficiency has powerful motivational properties.

In a similar manner, imbalance acts as both a signal and an activating experience in our lives. As one encounters the experience of imbalance (nebulous and unclear as the experience may be), there exists a drive to thwart the imbalance and attain a state of reduced tension.

Let's unpack this reasoning in a bit more detail. All of us live with imbalance, and realize that some level of imbalance is simply part of existing in a real world. Yet, perceived imbalance, as the name implies, connotes disequilibrium and tension. How much is tolerable? Of course it depends. It depends on the people involved, the unique personalities at hand, the sources of the tension, and the costs associated with the imbalance. Consequently, each of us has a threshold of imbalance we can handle and tolerate. Even that threshold shifts and sways given the explosion of life events. Yet when our perceived imbalance extends beyond this personal threshold, we encounter excess tension, and we are moved to action as a way to reduce this tension.

Conceptually, the imbalance and the accompanying tension act as an aversive motivational condition.[1] In part, this aversive condition is positive and functional. Often, it provides the motivation and energy to make needed changes and accomplish our lofty goals. However, most of us have experienced the point at which imbalance becomes stressful rather than inspirational; at this tipping point, imbalance has moved beyond a tolerable threshold and must be addressed. Interestingly, considerable research has supported the notion that people are prompted to pay attention to critical life needs when confronted with crisis.[2]

Let's quickly review our main points here. Perceived imbalance is important as a personal signal for attention, consideration, and change. And, perceived imbalance is important as an aversive motivational state that prompts us to action. Before going further, it is important to understand the nature of ones' perceptions of imbalance.

IMBALANCE

In our research, individual explanations of imbalance varied greatly, but two themes emerged. First, managers explained imbalance as veering from their personal determination of what really counted and was significant. As one female manager in a large international company noted:

> "Spending too much time on things that are not important. At the end of the day, when you think about it, did it really matter? . . .You lose sight of what's important. You get caught up in something . . . and it happens more at work when you get caught up in a project or little issue, and in the end, did it really matter?"

A second theme that surfaced views imbalance as a "perceived lack of control." Here, managers began to sense imbalance when they recognized an undesired loss of personal determination. Consider the following comments:

> "I like a lot of order. I like to know exactly kind of how things are going to play out. I like to know, I guess, the path down which I think things will go . . . (Imbalance occurs) when you feel that maybe your actions can't directly affect the outcome. . . . You know, of course, you don't have any control." (Mid-level manager of a regional hospital; female; early 30s)
> "If my life is out of balance, I feel like I'm out of control. You know, like my life is running me, and I'm not running my life." (Owner-manager of a small business; female; late 30s)

In summary, although people have trouble recognizing and defining balance, most people describe imbalance in ways that are consistent with the themes of significance and control. Further, imbalance is real; it is experienced viscerally, emotionally, and physically. Because it touches us at each of these three levels, it is an undeniable reality check. Behavior is not motivated by imbalance until we are brought face-to-face with the personal signals or cues of imbalance. So the journey toward balance begins here.

PERSONAL CUES OF IMBALANCE[3]

At the risk of recapitulation, let us suggest once again that the importance of balance is recognized most clearly when it is lost. We become aware of the need for balance when engulfed and overwhelmed by the vagaries of imbalance. With this in mind, it is important to possess an intrapersonal awareness or means of self-monitoring that signals the presence of imbalance. Understanding and unpacking these cues and signals is no simple task. However, in our research using intensive personal interviews, we have asked working managers and professionals to explain how they became aware of personal imbalance. We wanted to see if people were aware of personal cues, and we wanted to see if there were patterns or types of cues that were typically experienced.

In some cases, the awareness of personal cues, at least early cues, were either absent or ignored. Here, respondents admitted being well along the path of imbalance before recognizing that something was out of kilter. However, most respondents, no doubt drawing from experience over time, had learned to be sensitive and to pay attention to their personal cues of imbalance.

In our work, we are careful to emphasize the individualistic nature of the topic and we encourage managers and professional not to oversimplify their own experience by boxing themselves into convenient categories. Yet, for purposes of discussion, we uncovered five general types of personal cues.

Inner Emotional Tension

The first cue category of imbalance is "inner emotional tension." Note that while experiencing some tension, the tension is not seen as being displayed or expressed in any outward manner. Some managers described this cue simply as a feeling of "stress and tension," while others indicated a hard-to-define yet clear "lack of inner peace." Some managers even noted that their normal "joy of living" was mitigated. Importantly, respondents were often aware of this inner sensitivity or emotional tension before it was projected into overt action or stress-induced behavior. One manager noted that, "Everything seems to be more work than it used to be. . . . Even normally fun things become work."

General Moodiness

While the first cue deals with feelings of stress and heightened anxiety, the "general moodiness" cue represents a slightly more progressive effect since there was some degree of behavioral impact. Here, respondents noted that they "engaged in considerable amounts of worrying." One manager noted that she just become "fidgety." Respondents indicated being aware of this shift in mood even as it was occurring. This is a key point. Respondents were aware that their internal tension was becoming more apparent; perhaps it was not yet visibly apparent to others but it was increasingly difficult to deny to themselves.

Myopic Focus

A third personal cue is the emergence of a "myopic focus." This myopic focus occurs when the managers become overly occupied with particular tasks or experiences to the near-exclusion of all other areas of life. The myopic focus often manifests as a tendency to interpersonally disengage, as seen in the response of the following manager:

> "For me I think its when I find myself spending time thinking about something when my attention should be focused on something else. . . . You're at home . . . or maybe at dinner . . . and you're thinking and the other person is talking. And you're thinking, OK I have no idea what they just said because I've been focused on this problem, running it through my mind for the last ten minutes." (Mid-level manager of a regional hospital; female; early 30s)

A more extreme form of this myopic focus occurs when managers are so consumed by their work that they are unable to carry out regular activities that had previously been considered normal. In essence, they are temporarily immobilized by the demands of their myopic focus.

> "I get too overwhelmed with something. I will just almost not know what I should be doing next. I feel like I'm shuffling papers. I am doing things but not being productive in my work." (President of a mid-sized business; female; late 40s)

Lastly, the myopic focus also manifests itself in thought patterns rather than specific behaviors. Some of these patterns can be described humorously, as seen in the comments of the following highly successful female manager.

> "The on-the-path signals are little things. One is . . . clutter in the house, which drives me bonkers. . . . There are signals. I can see it happening. A pile of newspapers, somebody's shoes, or little things start to collect. And I can see the signals. They are in the not urgent, not important box for a little while there. You know, long enough then I get a physical feeling, the signal that life is out of balance when there is clutter in the house. When I walk into the house, or when I am not even in the house and I picture the house with little piles of clutter and shoes and things. And I get a physically adverse feeling of 'I wish I could fix that' . . . There is a very emotional feeling to me in being out of balance when I finally kinda hit the wall and think that pile of newspapers is going to send me to the psychiatrist." (Director in a large regional organization; female; late 30s)

Interestingly, this manager recognized, intellectually, that obsession with the clutter probably arose from a need to secure control and order in the midst of work or life-related confusion. Importantly, she had learned that when her focus on the clutter and associated feelings appeared, imbalance issues were now paramount.

Frustration and Anger

The fourth personal cue category is more overt and potentially damaging. Some managers noted that they became "angered more easily" than normal or had a "shorter fuse" or were more "quick tempered." Most respondents recognized these displays differed from their common or natural displays of emotion, noting that the true signal of imbalance was "acting out of character" or "getting angrier than usual." One manager recounted:

> "I feel angry . . . I feel like flying off the handle. . . . My fuse is shorter when it's usually a lot longer. . . . It definitely elevates the potential for conflict with whomever (a spouse, a child, or even a coworker) . . . it certainly elevates that. It has a trickle-down effect." (Mid-level manager in a large regional company; female; late 30s)

Physiological Responses

The fifth personal cue category is the presence of "physiological responses." In some cases, these responses are quite individualized and idiosyncratic. Yet, certain physiological responses are common and prevalent. In our studies, the most frequently mentioned cue, by far, was sleep disturbance. A typical respondent noted, "You know I'll be disturbed and wake up at 2 or 3 in the morning, and that's all I'm thinking about." The sleep cue evoked intensity since most respondents indicated that they were unable to disengage their minds and resume normal sleep activity. Other frequently mentioned behavioral cues, while not directly physiological but having physiological effects, were poor nutrition habits and the tendency to stop exercising.

An important and practical distinction is needed. The managers and professionals in our studies perceived the five themes above as cues that something was going on and needed to be addressed. These cues were so apparent to those experiencing them that some response was necessary, even if that response was a decision to delay, to do nothing and to "let it ride" for a while.

The experience of imbalance is always preceded by cues. Yet that does not mean that everyone is aware of the cues. Many people lack the sensitivity to fully acknowledge their personal cues for what they are and what they represent. In some cases these cues are even purposely dismissed in order to relieve the responsibility of addressing them. We want you to be sensitive to your personal cues. And, we want you to transmute these seemingly bothersome cues into springboards for action that move you toward recapturing balance.

PAYING ATTENTION

In general, we are optimists, but we are not naïve. As much as we recognize the importance of centering on personal cues of imbalance, this is not a natural activity in the whirlwind of life. We work with people who are busy and feel they have little time. Perhaps you fit this pattern. Paying attention, if it takes the form of one more thing on the "to do" list, is not an option.

Fortunately, the simple act of paying attention may provide a wealth of data even though it "costs" little in terms of time. In fact, using this technique actually requires that you are active, because it rests upon the signals you receive as feedback from your actions. Yet, learning to see and read personal cues is a practice that must be honed. Each of us already has the fundamental building blocks for this skill. For example, you recognize the cues in others. Chances are, you know when a spouse has had a bad day the moment he or she walks in the door. However, it is interesting, but very human, that we discount this same data when it relates to ourselves.

So, the first step is to simply pay attention to the data. What data, you ask? You are receiving data all the time, literally. In any given moment, it comes in the forms of impressions and feelings, reactions from colleagues and clients, interactions or lack of interactions with loved ones. And, of course, it comes from the signals and cues we discussed above. It is all there, but it is locked out of your consciousness or overwhelmed by all of the other happenings to which you feel you must attend. Consequently, you either miss or dismiss the data. You stifle or block the cues. You miss all this data by choosing not to pay attention. You dismiss when you have paid attention (either by force or happenstance) and choose to justify and rationalize your current course rather than use the data to take needed corrective actions.

We see this often when helping managers interpret their 360-degree feedback results. At times, managers are literally shocked by the comments of their peers and subordinates. We are frequently caught by the discomforting disconnect between one's self appraisals and that of key organizational compatriots. Recently, we sat with a young leader who was staggered by the blunt reality of the commentary he had just received. He seemed like a kind, even a gentle soul, who cared deeply for others and, at least in our workshops, demonstrated high levels of respectful interpersonal skill. Yet, his peers and subordinates at work described him as an obsessive hard driver whose push for success frequently included harsh and demeaning actions toward others. Almost sadly, he pleaded his case. "That's not the way I really am," he offered. How did he miss it?

We consoled him by agreeing that this may not be the "way he really is" and offering that such behavior was inconsistent with what we (and others) had seen in our weeks together. Yet, there was harsh reality he needed to consider.

Something in his behavior led those he worked with most closely to view him as cold, arrogant, and insensitive. He reasoned that the pressures of the job forced him primarily to attend to results alone, and he acquiesced that he gave people little time and attention. He also gave himself little time and attention, for if he had, he would have caught what he was doing before seeing it in black and white.

Most of the managers we work with miss or dismiss the data for a very understandable reason. It is laden with impressions and feelings of anxiety, reactions from colleagues and clients that are lacking, and interactions with loved ones that are not fulfilling. If this is what paying attention produces, why would anyone do it? While understandable, such a mindset reinforces the tendency to ignore the data, and accordingly robs you of precious information. Hear this: you will NEVER experience balance unless you pay attention, even though your initial attempts at paying attention produce anxiety. Paying attention gives you the data you need to show you if you are in fact, on track.

Not only does ignoring this data hamper your movement toward balance, ignoring it has additional consequences. Perhaps without your knowing it, you are expending energy by hiding this data from your awareness. The feelings and impressions received from the work you are doing are not distinct from the actual work you are doing. Rather, feelings and impressions are a part of whatever you are engaging in at any given moment, although a subjective and personal part. You may feel that holding this information to the side allows you to focus on what is "important." Or, you may feel that pushing this information aside is the strong and stoic response of a seasoned business leader. No matter why it is held aside, it consumes energy to do so.

We see evidence of dismissing the data in many of the managers we work with, as they turn to easy resolution. They plead, "Give me more time. Give me more resources. Let me reprioritize my workday. Help me avoid anything extraneous." Yet, the path to balance begins by experiencing these feelings and impressions and ultimately grappling with the discomfort of imbalance.

For most people, learning to pay attention often begins by attending to the subtle awareness that some change or modification seems needed. In other words, vague as it might be, you have a sense that all is not quite right. Perhaps it is a subtle shift in attitude or closeness with a loved one. Or, it is the slight downturn in the corners of your mouth as you turn the car off once arriving at work. Or, it is the discomfort you experience as you leave the structured environment of the office to return to a more confusing home life.

As you continue to pay attention, awareness becomes more salient. You begin to be aware not only when things are wrong, but when things are quite right. And, at an even deeper level, you learn to discern which pieces of the same situation are quite right, and which are not.

Consider this example. Some of the more mature and balanced executive couples we have interviewed have demonstrated this capacity for awareness of both balance and imbalance. They have also learned to use the information gained to make the slight adjustments needed to maintain balance. One couple has recounted daily time, taken both individually and collectively as a couple, to explore and discuss what is going on in their lives and how that feels to them. We use "feels" deliberately. It is important that their dialogue is less focused upon finding answers than it is upon listening and encouraging expression. (Most people find their answers in the process of honest expression and not from the process of problem solving.) The important element here is that both spouses experience the awareness and then make meaning of the awareness. The significant other is simply a concerned and trusted partner who supports its expression.

Begin your quest for balance by paying attention. But, paying attention to the data and cues is only a first step. Awareness of cues is a prompt, an initial stage of heightened personal awareness. While many people stop here, having lost the will to fight the ever-oppressive battle of imbalance, there is another crucial step, a stage of processing and contemplating. This stage, reflection, is discussed next.

REFLECTION

Reflection is quiet time, personal time, time spent focused inward, rather than outward. It helps us to determine what in our current life situation is producing the moodiness, the sleeplessness, or the frustration that are cues to imbalance. While finding these answers may provide the satisfaction of explanation, it does not lead to transformation. Taking reflection one step further is often necessary.

When we probe more deeply, reflection becomes a period of immersing ourselves in a search for meaning. Reflection requires that we grapple with the discomfort of life imbalance and it demands self-confrontation as a means of generating self-awareness.

Given this, it is no wonder why many managers and executives we have worked with resist this. When we suggest that a period of self-reflection is in order, excuses abound as to why a few hours are not available for this crucial task, particularly when executives realize that there are no tangible outcomes after the time is spent! As these excuses begin to surface, one of my favorite stories to tell is a lesson not learned from an executive, but from a trail run in late summer 2003. I was running along and feeling as if I had the stamina and the energy to pick up my pace. As I tried to increase my speed, something felt off. I tried to breathe differently, strike the trail differently with my heel, pull my shoulders back . . . nothing was producing that "click" that helps a runner find his or her groove. And, as I tried to self-correct while running, I kept feeling more and more off. My attempts were actually slowing my pace! I then came to a break in the trail where runners must cross a road. There are rarely cars here, but this particular day, I was forced to stop for a black Toyota Camry. When I resumed running, it did click, automatically and without effort. I ran the rest of my route, at top speed, enjoying the crisp morning. The lesson? Sometimes you must stop completely in order to find a new rhythm. Self-reflection, although sometimes done on the fly, may require a full and complete stop. If your attempts to create feelings of balance while in the midst of the full-court press of life have not produced results, let us be your Toyota Camry. Stop, and pay attention.

Unless you are facing a crisis, personal or professional, the draw to stop completely and dedicate time for reflection is likely not very strong. Just as it takes us a few days to settle in to the relaxed pace of a vacation, it takes time to settle in to the quiet, spacious time you may dedicate for reflection. If you are inspired to do some personal reflection as you read the rest of this book, we ask that you trust those minutes and hours of settling in. Don't rush to resume work on the many projects you may have. Rather, dedicate yourself to the time allotted, be it three hours or three days, and let go of any pressing responsibility. Your job during this allotted time is to reflect. And if you have done so, regardless of what the outcome of your reflection time may be, you have done your job.

Let us help you. The appendix contains thoughts, questions, and writing exercises that may guide you during these periods of reflection. You may also reflect upon phrases, interactions, or "a-ha!" moments from your own experiences.

ANOTHER LOOK BEFORE YOU LEAP

"I've got to be honest. This isn't where I thought we'd be headed. You seem to be arguing that balance is an inner-focused process rather than a set of actions. Why?"

Ultimately, balance will require you to take a series of carefully weighed actions; it is an active, not a passive process. But knowing which actions to take, which steps will bring you closer to balance cannot be determined without a period of reflection. Many popular books skip this step; they provide the "Top Ten Ways to Regain Balance." Shorten your commute. Take a vacation. Call your mother. We do not agree with this approach; we do not agree that taking action is appropriate until you know what is right for you. For instance,

I may use my commute to listen to books on CD. An avid reader with limited time in the evenings to sit down with a book, this may be the way I integrate this important piece into my busy life. Following a suggestion to shorten my commute, without considering its balance-producing effects, actually works against my sense of balance.

As some people experience imbalance, they strive to do more—a pattern that reinforces the need for activity, but not the need for meaning. It reminds us of the proverbial definition of insanity: doing the same thing over and over again and expecting a different result. The way to break this cycle is through reflection, and using the wisdom gained through reflecting to do something different.

We want you to focus outward, but not yet. There is a deliberate and some-what disciplined process that enhances the likelihood of reaching the balance you seek. Short-circuiting this process may lead to some stop-gap, feel good solutions. But they will stop short of ultimate meaning, because your actions are not informed by your core self. Discovering the core self is the work of the next chapter.

NOTES

1. The argument presented in the early part of this chapter draws heavily on dissonance theory.

2. For example, see Charles R. Stoner and John F. Gilligan, *The Adversity Challenge: How Successful Leaders Bounce Back From Setbacks* (Provo, UT: Executive Excellence Publishing, 2002).

3. Our previous work has been summarized here. See Charles R. Stoner, Jennifer Robin, and Lori Russell-Chapin, "On the Edge: Perceptions and Responses to Life Imbalance," *Business Horizons* 48 (2005): 337–46.

Chapter Six

Digging a Hole to China

Balance cannot be obtained without attending to who we really are: our core self. Stated simply, choices made when the core self is the driving or motivating force are more likely to create the experience of balance.

There is little novelty to this perspective. Most thoughtful writing on life balance has emphasized the centrality of one's core self, although the language may differ slightly. We have already discussed the significant work done by Friedman and Greenhaus.[1] These authors stressed, as their first principle of action for achieving balance, clarifying what is important. Of course, this clarification requires a personal awareness and grasp of one's values and life priorities. The ground-breaking work of Joan Kofodimos offered only slightly different phrasing. She argued that one of the keys to integrating balance in our lives was "developing awareness of our real self values and aspirations."[2]

Continuing the theme, Fuller offered a broader life perspective. He noted that "by middle adulthood it becomes apparent that we cannot accomplish an infinite number of things in a single lifetime. There will always be unfinished tasks, new roads to travel, new possessions to acquire. Thus, what is needed is some kind of perspective from which to sort out and arrange life's many opportunities and experiences into some kind of pattern that will reveal which ones are ultimately worth pursuing."[3] We believe that the mechanism for "sorting it all out" rests in awareness and understanding of one's core self. Fuller continues by asserting that "to feel healthy and satisfied (what we refer to as balanced) humans require not a tensionless state such as is provided by satiating our physical needs, but rather an active striving or struggling toward some worthy goal."[4] Again, we believe that this sense of worthy goal resides in the core self.

72

Consistent with research in the life balance arena, we have argued that balance is only partially a time issue and an energy issue. It is more fully a *meaning* issue. It moves into focus as you unravel who you are and what gives you purpose. It is a step that requires us to dive deep. Kushner suggests that "we can be so busy taking care of things that we neglect our souls." He argues that ". . . we need to rely on the wisdom of the soul to guide our working and living hours . . . Especially when I am busy, I need to define myself by some thing other than my work, lest I lose part of my soul in the process."[5]

The question is of the utmost importance. What does it mean to realize one's core self—the real, authentic core self? Authenticity does not reside in what someone tells us. Neither does it depend on what society nor cultural norms expect us to be. Authenticity is what you must be because it is the purest expression of who you are.

Frequently, we pursue images of ourselves that have value for others. These images have value to the corporation. They have value to the family. They have value to the community, to society, to history. And while these images may coincide with your own core self, they often do not do so completely. You may be pursuing others' expectations of you, coming up empty and wondering why. The pursuit of others' expectations rarely brings you the sense of balance you desire. It follows that in order to obtain balance, one must truly know this core self.

WHAT I DO AND WHAT I AM

Most of us confuse the distinction between what we do and who we are. In many ways, for many of us, the former defines and molds the latter. The work we do unfolds as an array of expanding expectations, and we compartmentalize ourselves, becoming mere prototypes of our work. When what we do limits or restricts the expression of what we are, a natural sense of imbalance is experienced. Many of the people with whom we have worked allow the job title and job description to confine and restrict which of their myriad skills, abilities, and characteristics are considered relevant. Sadly, trapped in an ever-deepening pattern, these people stifle the expression of their true gifts, place frustrating limits on their potential, and experience emotional pangs of imbalance. Realize that these professionals are not intentionally limiting or restricting themselves or the expression of their gifts; most intelligent humans do not actively engage in such self-maligning behavior. However, if one does not know the depth or content of his or her core self, an unfortunate side-effect is a constricted self-definition. And not surprisingly, that which we know best—often our work—becomes the base of measurement and the gauge of what seems reasonable and appropriate.

Now let's be clear. What we do will always affect what we are. As Merton noted, "Every moment and every event of every man's life on earth plants something in his soul."[6] Clearly, the twisting, often uncharted path of what we do carves and alters our character. Further, such shaping can be an expansive, growing emancipation of who and what we are. In such a context, the work we do releases and excites and challenges and energizes.

However, all too often, a darker shadow is cast. What we do prods and pushes us in undesired directions. (Paid work is only one of many culprits; others may include civic, volunteer, and family responsibilities). The pattern of activity moves so steadily and insidiously that we are generally unaware of the approaching tipping point until it has been crossed. Listen to the expression of this breach, as recounted by a highly-regarded executive in his early 40s:

"Just a short 7 months or so ago I was suffering from burnout . . . traveling 1–3 nights a week and putting in 4–7, 20-hour days a week. I was managing some 40 people in 5 different businesses in two states on 24 hour shifts. My family life was suffering as was my health, and I definitely had that hopeless 'floating on a raft in the ocean' feeling. I was throwing up all the flags until finally one day I told my boss I was scheduling back surgery that I could put off no longer. This was how I was going to get a break. I needed the surgery, mind you, but I welcomed back surgery at this point—that is how desperate I was. I thought that this would be the end of the multiple-state work overload crisis for awhile. To my surprise 2 days after surgery I found myself at home getting calls and taking them, participating in meetings and working 10 hours a day during the following 2 months while on disability from surgery.

To make a long story short . . . I thought I finally found the end to this madness when one day talking with a peer, this manager had just gotten the same bonus, made the same salary or more, and had all the same successes I had . . . yet he worked 8 hours a day at one site with only a handful of people working for him. Wow, did this seem like an insult to me after all my hard work . . . I felt . . . well I'm sure you know how I felt. His statement to me was learn to close the laptop, leave it at work because no matter how much you do, there will always be that much more there the next day. I don't know that I buy into that theory 100%, but it did wake me up to the fact that I was killing myself for little or no benefit and in fact dragging my family life into the gutter as well. I feel I may have finally found that happy medium between work and home for now. I have finally off-loaded the out of state site I had to manage and basically cut my work load in half. I do know when to shut the laptop and say enough. I hope I can keep with it as I am a type A personality and definitely have a tendency to just suck it up and suffer when work calls . . . One day maybe I will find that peaceful . . . job. . . . when I retire."

The language and images are intriguing and somewhat frightening, but they are not unique. That "floating on a raft in the ocean feeling" that is described could be an apt expression for many of those we have studied and with whom we have worked. The manifestations - psychological, behavioral, and physiological - are idiosyncratic, but the feeling is not. The emotion being expressed is imbalance.

In our view, work is viewed as a context for experiencing, enhancing, and expressing what and who we are and what we are becoming. This need not detract from or obscure the pursuit of excellence at work. In fact, professionals who have wholly invested their evolving core selves in work are those who provide deep and meaningful organizational contributions. These individuals experience a sense of commitment to and engagement in their work, and rightfully so, as their work is their context for creating a life of meaning.[7]

We are about to embark upon a discussion of a concept fundamental and crucial to our notion of balance. In many ways, it is the gateway to creating a life of meaning. This gateway is knowledge of your core self. It may be helpful to consider this in a larger frame, using the ideas of the great philosopher Spinoza to help us elucidate what you are about to do next.

In a wonderful and classic metaphor, Spinoza suggests that an apple tree flourishes when given the appropriate ecological conditions: light, temperature, air quality, and water. Further, when these conditions appear in the ideal proportion, the tree becomes what it is meant to be, and produces fruit it is meant to produce. However, no matter how perfectly the ecological conditions match those required by the apple tree, it will never produce pears. While the apple tree is endowed with the potential to produce wonderfully delicious apples, that potential must be carefully cultivated to be realized. And, while the apple tree does not have the capability to produce any other fruit, it is still complete in its purpose. To focus on what the tree cannot do is not only unrealistic, but diminishes our sense of pleasure in what it can.[8]

To extend his metaphor, your core self is the tree and its produce. You must know what it is you are uniquely qualified to accomplish, and the likely fruits of your labors. In the next chapter, we discuss the ecological conditions, or your life situation, and how to bring your life situation in line with your gifts and purpose. Yet, just as we do not know the appropriate conditions for a tree until we know what species of tree it is, we do not know our appropriate, balance-producing life situation until we know our core self. Thus, while two tasks lie before you, the first must be discovering your core self.

REVEALING THE CORE SELF

We argue that the core self is recognized and understood through two aspects: one's purpose and one's gifts. One's purpose is that deep personal sense of unique significance. *Purpose* is what provides us worth and meaning. Consequently, one's purpose can never be fulfilled by another because it requires a certain constellation of talents, life experiences, and skills that are inimitable. And, incidentally, the constellation of talents, life experiences, and skills comprise one's *gifts*, the other key component of the core self.

Purpose

Kouzes and Posner, in their superb primer, *The Leadership Challenge*, encourage leaders to "find their voice," which begins with a clarification of values. "You have to take a journey into those places in your heart and soul where you bury your treasures so that you can carefully examine them and eventually bring them out for display. You must know what you care about."[9] We believe that one's voice, when found, speaks of purpose.

We have found it fascinating to challenge our workshop participants to explore and articulate their purpose. Understandably and appropriately, some participants resist, arguing that their purpose is in flux and accordingly fuzzy and unclear. We agree that one's life purpose is ever-evolving and more will be said about this later in this chapter. However, the more important perspective is not to probe some future-oriented, idealized culmination of life purpose. Instead, we focus on the here and now. What is your purpose today? What is the base from which you are living? Meaning and purpose are best viewed in the now, not in some grand life scheme. We repeat the words of Frankl here for emphasis. "What matters, therefore, is not the meaning of life in general, but rather the specific meaning of a person's life at a given moment."[10]

Interestingly, some people have personally meaningful responses to the question of purpose. For example, one business leader noted that his purpose was to build a work environment where people felt "respected and engaged; where they (his organizational members) feel good about themselves and the work they do." Importantly, this purpose extended beyond work, and defined the way he approached all interactions and lived his life.

One young professional was challenged by our question and embarked upon a great deal of reflection. She reported to us that she discovered her purpose was "to be a mirror in which people see their own beauty while also supporting them in their journey to become the most honest, authentic expression of who they are." Importantly, she knew she had tapped into her core self, as her stated purpose permeated all facets of life. In her friendships, in her work as a counselor, in her interactions with her students, and in her family, her aim was to help people realize both their uniqueness and their potential.

Recognize the similarity of these examples. In each case, purpose extended beyond one realm of life (work, family, personal) and encapsulated the individual's sense of personal significance. Also, it is important to note that purpose has an outward effect upon others and or the environment. In both examples, the professionals articulated ways in which their lives were to touch or improve the lives of others.

While these people and others are able to offer powerful statements of personal purpose, these articulations are certainly not the norm. It can be rather overwhelming to jump right in and try to define one's life purpose. Many of us, when confronted with such a penetrating query, exhibit a deer-in-the-headlights gaze and plead ignorance of where to turn. We may even take it one step further, contending that these are not questions for the common business professional and are better left to the philosophers. This reaction is not surprising, particularly given that the answer to the question of purpose does not reveal itself without searing personal reflection. Once people have engaged in this reflection, though, their lives begin to make sense on a grander scale. They not only experience meaning and balance on a regular basis, they are able to choose life experiences that engage this purpose and further their sense of meaning.

To ease the process of revealing purpose and recognizing what is at your core, we begin by asking you to determine what is not at your core. That is, determining who you are not. This is a thorny exercise, but we find that many people find it much easier to articulate what they do not want than to describe precisely all they desire. For example, sitting across the table from an executive in the midst of a career change, we attempted to help him understand which potential careers would capitalize upon his core self. Although he was unsure how to respond, he was quite clear regarding what he did not want in this career. Having lived the experience of 15-hour days and constant travel, he adamantly rejected these options. Although this did not get us any closer to determining which career he should pursue, it narrowed our options in suggesting those he should. In other words, while this exercise did not define his core self, it provided important data needed to aid in the process. This executive enumerated critical boundary conditions, and vowed to stay within these parameters. When asked, "Why?" the executive got a glimpse of his core. It suggested a key component of his core self was the meaning of family and his commitment to guard against being singularly absorbed by his work at the family's expense.

Consider another example. Another young executive had built a successful career by exceeding all organizational expectations. She was typically the first in the door, volunteered for high profile assignments, proposed creative initiatives, and immersed herself in being the "ideal" employee. Interestingly, upon reflection, she began to understand that these behaviors and accomplishments failed to provide real meaning for her. All that she was doing and achieving was not really her life's purpose. While she wasn't quite certain who she was, it did become more clear what she was not. She began to understand that the more technical dimensions of her job—an area where she excelled—offered little intrinsic reward. Rather, it carried with it the cost of missed opportunity to pursue more interpersonally focused endeavors. Importantly, she understood what was not part of her core self, and further understood that making a direct and immediate impact upon others was her purpose. Not surprisingly, this realization culminated in a career change.

Note that this process is cumulative and non-linear. Knowing who you are not will help you determine who you are, and knowing who you are will help you decipher who you are not. We refer to this as our reduction/expansion approach. By reducing the options, one can expand his or her understanding of what is really there. What we are suggesting is not a whole new skill set necessary to proceed on the quest for knowing one's core. We engage in this reduction/expansion thinking regularly and naturally in our day to day lives. In fact, our editor came up with a beautiful example of how this operates. You are preparing for dinner. You look in the freezer to see what is there. There is not a package of pork chops or ground beef; there is only chicken. The options have been reduced—chicken is what's for dinner. But, now you can begin the expansion steps. What shall be done with the chicken? It can be marinated or grilled or baked into a casserole. The options are limitless. By first understanding what is not available and fully accepting what is (reduction), we can then begin creative thinking about what is possible (expansion).

At this point, it is useful and important for you to consider what you are not, what you do not want, where you do not want to go. Please don't shy away from or dismiss this important reflective activity. Be specific, and concrete. Try to divorce yourself from expectations of others, your current life situation, and your history.

Again, some examples may be helpful. For instance, one workshop participant indicated, "I do not want to be an absentee father who misses his children's youth." Once this first realization was brought forward, we asked, "Why is this not a part of you?" The answer to this question, though often stated in a clumsy and imprecise manner, becomes a critical and revealing clue for what is at his core. It is also a clue to what was sabotaging his sense of balance. Continuing to probe, we found that he took his role as a father seriously and did not wish to sacrifice his fulfillment of it for anything, even that much sought-after promotion.

This process, while seemingly simple, can become complex, particularly at times when that which is not at our core is manifested in our day-to-day behaviors and attitudes. Consider the example of Mark. Mark came to our workshop labeled a "problem child." Quiet, contemplative, and reserved, he could also be explosive and abrasive, particularly when projects were approaching deadlines and the stress level was high. Although he was technically competent, he ran roughshod over people, ignored their feelings, and showed every appearance of being cold and insensitive. Mark understood his effect on people. He was puzzled, because at his core, he knew he was not that "uncooperative and disrespective colleague" that his staff and peers so often saw. Rather, throughout his career he recalled his profound sense of gratitude for the contributions of others, and he knew his work was impossible without others' contributions and support. Mark eventually came to realize that given the pressure-cooker demands of his current job, he would probably never be able to reveal his true core self. It will come as no surprise that his work was a draining, rather than energizing experience for him.

As in the case of Mark, your purpose and therefore the answers to these questions may be disguised by circumstance and habit. We encourage you to persist in your quest for discovery. By engaging in this exercise, you are slowly peeling away the superficial layers surrounding who you really are. Follow this further. When you determine one aspect of who you are, use it to illuminate another aspect of who you are not. Again, be specific and ask yourself "Why?" Once you hit a dead end, begin again, with a new answer to the first question, "What things are not a part of me?" Realize that this is a multi-event process. You are not going to sit down on Friday evening between commercials and knock out these heady answers. Rather, you will struggle with one piece, perhaps for days, often feeling that there is limited progress . . . until one day you realize you have the answer. If it was matter of *creating* your core self, you could block out two days in your schedule and have a final product by noon on Wednesday. (Those of you enamored with strategic planning are salivating now.) But, you are not engaged in a creative process; instead you are engaged in the process of *revealing* your core self, and more specifically, revealing your purpose. This is an iterative process of finding what is already there, but has been hidden, blocked, or pushed off center-stage. Even more paradoxical, the process is not only iterative, it is without a definitive end point, as your purpose is always evolving. Again, we draw from the rich insights of Thomas Merton, "What we are is to be sought in the invisible depths of our own being. . ."[11]

Gifts

Gifts, as stated above, are the unique talents, competencies, skills, perspectives, life experiences, and world-view that make us who we are. Accordingly, gifts are the most pragmatic, natural, uplifting means by which we fulfill our purpose.

Recently we worked with Liz, an amazing woman whose capacity to listen to people, understand their needs, and move with conviction and compassion was truly inspiring. We immediately recognized her ability in connecting and building confidence in others. Did this gift come naturally or had it been developed over years of practice? In all likelihood, both her fundamental personality and the shaping effects of life's experiences played a role. What we did know was that in the human resource arena of her organization, through her leadership in her church, and through her supportive involvement with family and friends, her gifts were activated and exercised. She was a difference maker reaching a noble purpose.

Liz is not unique. In working with managers and executives, we have met a number of individuals who have found ways to define and orient their lives (work and nonwork) to provide ample opportunities for expressing and capitalizing on their unique gifts. In nearly all cases, these individuals reported experiencing meaning and balance.

Not only are gifts a gateway to achieving meaning and balance, it is the blocking of one's gifts or the inability or unwillingness to use those gifts that prompt and exacerbate feelings of imbalance. This view is not new, and it is supported by research. For example, it has been known for quite some time that the experience of underutilization is a significant stressor.[12] In other words, not having the opportunity to use the talent and skill (and in our terms, gifts) is a major cause of psychological dysfunction.[13] Thus, if not to ultimately use these discoveries to achieve meaning and balance, examining and assuring the utilization of one's gifts can be a means to psychological health.

All of this may seem painfully obvious, but we believe it does warrant frank discussion. We have encountered too many people who simply do not recognize the powerful gifts at their core. We've coached managers who pine for abilities to make tough decisions and do so devoid of emotional involvement. They wish to engage their rational thinking, come to a conclusion, and then move on. Yet, at their core, they have intense regard for people, relationships, harmony, and camaraderie. By fighting to be what they are not, they disown the fragile and rare interpersonal gift of building powerful relationships with others—a much-needed commodity in most high pressure, competitive environments.

Recent research and thinking has emphasized the merit of maximizing one's strengths rather than developing one's weaknesses as a means to full leadership development.[14] These studies note that self-development efforts have been skewed for much too long, focusing the successful professional's time and energy on all of those things he or she is not. While we agree that fatal flaws need to be addressed, professionals must ultimately lead from their strengths rather than their areas for development.

In other cases, gifts are recognized, but individuals choose not to engage them, usually out of fear of the image that would be projected if the gift is actualized. For example, the executive mentioned earlier refused to accept his natural sensitivity because he did not want to appear "weak." In other cases, gifts are blocked by one's current circumstance. For example, individuals may be in jobs that require tough decision making to the exclusion of opportunities for connection. It is important to realize that one's current circumstance is a product of one's choices. And these choices may have been made while denying or minimizing one's gifts. Thus, it is important to know what your unique gifts are as we move forward.

In the exercises dealing with purpose, you may have already noticed that some of what you have uncovered can be very easily seen as your gifts. Now, we will explore this theme more directly. We would like you to consider, "What are your gifts?" What are those gifts that are uniquely yours, gifts that you both possess and have used? Don't be shy, and don't pretend that you do not have gifts. We all do, but most of us spend more time lamenting the gifts we wish we had rather than experiencing, appreciating, using, and enhancing those we do.

ENGAGING YOUR CORE

Once you are aware of your unique gifts, the next thing we'd ask would be to identify those places in your life where they are being used. What is the impact of this? By impact, we mean, how does that affect you? And, how does it affect others? One senior executive, president of his own company, had built a rich consulting practice catering to top executive teams. However, his passion was working one-on-one with junior executives who were emerging as leaders. This mentoring process allowed him to use his special talents and gain satisfaction that he was making a difference. He experienced the flood of fulfillment that you have felt when your gifts are released. We have found consistently that those who engage their own gifts (rather than those they feel they "ought" to project) have the greatest sense of personal significance and meaning. If you are honest with yourself, it is this feeling that moves you and creates passionate living. We argue that when your gifts are released and used in pursuit of your purpose, you are evoking the essential nature of your core self.

Instead of taking our word for it, though, recall a personal experience. How did you feel when you had the opportunity to engage your core self? This is your point of reference. When you feel awash with fulfillment, be aware of what is happening and why it is happening. Pay attention. This is the glimpse of your purpose, gifts, and core self, and the clearest path you will know to balance and meaning.

There is one final question regarding your gifts. What gifts you are not using? There are two possible reasons for latent or inactive gifts. First, you may find yourself in a situation where you do not have the opportunity to release your gifts; we have already discussed this scenario. Second, you may find yourself in a situation in which the expression of your gifts is actively punished or ridiculed (either implicitly or explicitly). For example, one executive we know has deftly created a supportive subculture in his area of his organization. He is an optimist, free with well-deserved praise, and openly encouraging of his staff. Although his people appreciate his rather nurturing leadership approach, the organizational leaders to whom he reports neither respect nor reinforce his style. In fact, they deride and minimize his value to the organization. In their eyes, he has taken a soft approach and therefore his eye is not intently on the bottom line. Ironically, the loss of respect and credibility reverberates through his staff. The initiatives and programs they wish to put in place with his guidance and positive feedback are often stalled further up the chain of command. The result has not been minor. He does not sleep well; he does not eat well; he has become forgetful and anxious at work, further reinforcing the perceptions of upper management. Clearly, he struggles and experiences discontent and imbalance largely because his uniqueness is thwarted by this particular organization.

If you have underutilized gifts, and they can be identified, what do you do? How do you engage your gifts? Our answer: test them to see if they produce the feelings of fulfillment described above. We have encouraged countless managers to take this approach. Conversations with superiors may be needed to explain what you would like to do and how you would like to contribute within the organization. The same is true for non-work or family relationships. Negotiations may need to ensue with a spouse or significant other in order to redistribute shared responsibilities. In fact, sometimes the best venue in which to "try on" the once hidden gifts may be a safe environment, which may not always be the environment in which you wish to ultimately evoke the gift. Volunteer or community activities are a common venue we suggest. In fact, one of the advantages people find in attending our balance workshop is the opportunity to explore and tap their underutilized gifts. Directive managers become reflective and thoughtful when off-site. Shy managers assertively share their views in a way their coworkers would find uncharacteristic. Results-driven executives support and nurture their fellow workshop participants. On the job, these behaviors would be too far out of character and too uncomfortable to release, but among the other participants, managers have license to express these characteristics.

For example, one manager in her mid-30s was frustrated by the restrictive, rather non-creative demands of her job. She felt her need to positively affect others in creative ways was totally blocked by her organization. She sought expression of her gifts elsewhere. One avenue was to teach at a local university in the evenings. On the surface, all of the pieces fit together. However, she found the process restrictive. She did not enjoy the interactions with students to the extent she had imagined. She found the rigors of class preparation and grading mind-numbing. This was not, however, a failed excursion. She had new data and she recognized this was not the vehicle for expression she sought.

As her coach, we encouraged her to attempt to forge helping relationships at work. She proposed a mentoring program, and she facilitated "lunch and learns" for new professionals. Through these means, she created new routes of expression for her gifts. In turn, she gave engaged value to her organization, and felt the contentment of personal balance. Again, we illustrate that balance is realized through the expression of your special gifts.

Of course, some organizations may not see the value in these programs and block their progress. Then, another decision route must be pursued. Again, a blunted course is not failure. It is simply more information—a choice eliminated. The balance you seek clearly lies somewhere else. Make no mistake, as more and more extracurricular routes are eliminated, one's career decision may become weighty. At the extreme, a whole new organization or career may be sought. But, this is not without all of the data gained in exploring other routes and the satisfaction of knowing all options had been considered.

Note that looking for expression of gifts outside of work may appear to simply be adding more demands to an already harried schedule. However, if you buy in to this, you are working from a traditional set of assumptions. Balance is only partially and we believe minimally about time. There is always time to do what one really wants to do and commits to do. We have rarely found people who are engaged in activities that tap their gifts who are fatigued and despondent. You will know when your gifts are engaged; it creates as much if not more energy than it expends. As David Whyte recounted, "The antidote to exhaustion is wholeheartendness."[15]

We need to extend this theme. We have all experienced moments, days, or weeks when we were working feverishly on something we believed in. In the process, we felt we were in the "flow." Eighteen hour days were not overwhelming and consuming. Rather, they were filled with energy and meaning. Understandably, such a schedule cannot be perpetuated forever, but the energy one derives living from unique purpose and gifts is life-giving. Note, also, that these times likely came either when significant others in life were either completely supportive of the cause, or at times when their conflicting concerns and wishes for us were not expressed. It is at these times when it is easiest to act from our core self, rather than being seduced or bound by the expectations of others. If it strikes you that these expressions seem deviant from traditional thinking on life balance, thinking that prescribes and limits us into carefully construed time frames, you are exactly right.

EVOLUTION: BEING AND BECOMING

Let's review. The core self is comprised of the gifts (talents) you possess and your core life purpose. We have observed and heard from those with whom we have worked and interviewed that it is tough to experience balance if the expression of our gifts and purpose is thwarted by our current situation. Conversely, situations that permit us to utilize our gifts and fulfill our purpose provide the foundations from which balance flourishes.

However, simply experiencing an existing synchronization between the requirements of our current situation and the expression of our gifts and purpose is a far too limiting view of balance for complex, evolving people. Accordingly, a more dynamic view of core self must include both a current and a potential dimension.

Understandably, the co-existence of a present and future perspective of core self may be difficult to conceive as well as a difficult thing to put into practice. For example, many professionals have experienced work situations that allow them opportunities for expressing their present personal gifts and purpose, but thwart their efforts to grow and expand. As such, these professionals have locked themselves into their present synchronization. Such a state of affairs is not hard to rationalize. When we are experiencing balance, we want to stay there. Yet, people evolve. Paradoxically, then, staying in balance comes from constant movement, not from staying put. For example, the job that seemed so exciting and challenging, exactly what you wanted and needed when you were 25 and single, no longer seems to provide the opportunity to express your gifts in service of realizing your purpose just a few years later.

Let's extend our new way of thinking about balance. Balance has both being and becoming dimensions. Being is where we are now and how that context aligns with our gifts and purpose. Becoming is allowing ourselves to grow, evolve, and experience an enriched portrait of our dynamic gifts and unfolding purpose. The bottom line: if the contents of our core self, our purpose and gifts, don't evolve, we get stuck, we stagnate, and we stifle our natural need for maturity.

The Freedom to Become

The first step in honoring the becoming is to allow yourself the freedom to actually pursue a new path—a decision that is considerably more difficult than it may seem. Recall how difficult it actually is to break from the pattern of career-focused success. Recall how success fuels our sense of competence, control, and significance. Recall the infinite nature of these needs—gaining more of each does not satiate our longing. Instead, it sparks and drives us to pursue more and work harder to maintain and enhance what we have achieved.

Therefore, becoming may involve building a new paradigm, replete with new assumptions and new criteria. In short, we are defining a new purpose and meaning for our lives. Ideally, such refining of purpose is an ongoing process. Purpose is shaped, over time, by experience. Accordingly, every experience provides evidence that can be used for the shaping of our purpose.

Most of us redefine purpose when we are forced to do so. Typically, we are pushed and prodded to move off dead center and seriously reconsider our pursuits. The prompting or precipitating events can occur at any time. Some of these events arise externally, appearing quickly, such as a crisis. At other times, these events build slowly, over years, until we finally realize that the pain of not changing is simply too great. It is difficult to prescribe precisely what prompts a change. What is clear is that finally one begins to redefine themselves and the meaning of their lives.

It is conceivable that one will define and redefine their purpose and meaning a number of times though their adult lives. In fact, not doing so seems rather stilted and unrealistic. Some of the happiest, most contented people we know are those that have allowed themselves to be redefined - people who have culled new purpose and meaning from life's events and experiences.

In many cases, the path of becoming unfolds incrementally with unexpected turns and unwanted detours. Often a refined purpose is revealed through exclusion - we learn, through experience, to recognize pursuits which offer little personal meaning. Don't miss this point. There is no lost experience. If we are receptive, an experience can be shaping as it moves you to avoid a recurrence of that experience. Of course, rays of purpose may be sparked by encounters or experiences that push us to reflect and engage in deep consideration of what brings true meaning. Let's look at this a bit more closely.

As an academic, I am generally cautious of the young man or woman who sits in my office and outlines, in meticulous detail, their life plan for the next 20 years. At 18 years of age, how do they know? Yet, their parents are proud and most adults are duly impressed. I recently listened as one of these honor students explained that she was going to double major in business and political science; then she would attend law school, focusing on international law; upon graduation she would live in Europe for 2–3 years; she would return to practice for a large firm in Chicago, New York, Boston, or Washington, D.C.; and one day would become a judge.

Now it is impressive to have goals and targets and be aware of what is needed to reach those goals. But I can't help but wonder, whose meaning this really is? Is it a surprise that her father is a successful lawyer and her mother is a highly-regarded business executive?

Even more striking, I hope she does not continue blindly pursuing her educational goal if she experiences a lack of meaning in her study of law. I hope she does not neglect the excitement and warmth she feels when she volunteers at an inner-city shelter for neglected children. I hope she does not push away the urge that tells her that she has a special connection with children, particularly those at great risk. I hope she does not ignore the inner voice that tells her that her life of privilege is now to be repaid by serving those who are most vulnerable. I hope she will not squander the great gift of compassion and heart that emanate when she is with these special kids. I hope she can accept her fellow volunteer at the center; a young man whose background dramatically differs from hers. I hope she can see that as they laugh and drink coffee and talk about each child with whom they are working, she is falling in love. I hope she can rebel against the plan because her meaning seems so clearly to be guiding her in a new direction. Yet, I surmise she will not. She will persevere because it is expected. She will follow the plan because it would embarrass a lot of people not to do so. She will attain some notoriety and success. But will she have missed her true gifts? Will she ever realize that it's never too late? Can she take her new experiences and training and find a way to reach out? How will it all unfold?

You see, I'm more comfortable with the 18 year old freshman who says candidly, "I have no idea." I'm impressed with the 20 year old junior who says, "I don't know exactly what I will do, but I've learned a lot. I've got to do something that will affect society and help people and address some of the problems we have." I'm impressed with the graduate who says, "I'm going to work for this business and I'm excited, but this might not be where I end up."

Are these failures? Some would look at these examples with a suspicious eye. We prefer to say these are works in process, searching for meaning—defining and refining it as life unfolds. It is a healthy response.

It's not just the young that must be considered here. Some additional examples may be helpful. I recently was granted the opportunity to work with an outstanding group of successful leaders. Although my theme for this group centered around adversity and rebounding from the depths of crisis, the participants' inspirational exchanges spoke to the heart of balancing life and redefining meaning. One successful entrepreneur shared that her 70 hour workweek was staggered by the unexpected, terminal illness of her aging mother. Struggling to attend to her executive duties and meet the tug of family responsibilities, she finally realized that choices had to be made. She backed off her business schedule, delegated widely, and committed to making her mother's final months as full and rich as possible. In the process, she met other elderly women, and she recognized a sensitivity to their plight heretofore unbeknownst to her. She also recognized that her business background made her an effective advocate for this most needy population. Slowly, she began to see a new path unfolding—a path of social influence and activism. Today, she has sold her business and is committed to a new life direction. Although prompted by crisis and an emotional sense of duty, the shift in focus led to a redefining of meaning and purpose.

Another young manager discussed the bothersome squeeze of trying to balance her hectic business schedule with the demands of being a single mother with two young children at home. While she loved her boys dearly, she had also crafted a successful and promising career. The prospects of choosing between mutually exclusive options prompted both worry and general depression. It also prompted a time of deep personal probing, reflection, and insight. She finally realized that she could not "have it all."

She adjusted her schedule to accommodate her children. In the process, she stepped off the corporate fast track. However, she reasoned that such a move made sense "for now." Since she has never left the corporate arena, she hopes to return to a more active organizational role as her children mature. But that piece will unfold. She is still balancing and searching for the proper fit. However, she has a firm grounding in what is currently important and a clear sense of the parameters within which current choices must be set.

She has also recognized our fundamental perspective. Our search for meaning is ongoing and ever-changing, and accordingly balancing is an ongoing activity. Let's discuss this concept of balancing in the next chapter.

ANOTHER LOOK BEFORE YOU LEAP

"I work in the social services field and I see people using their gifts all the time. My colleagues all have passion for helping others: they secure resources and negotiate with the power companies to keep the lights on; they are the first call when mom has gone off her medications again; they provide countless hours of therapy and succor to families in need. It seems that all it buys them is burnout, not the balance you are speaking about."

The case management administrator was visibly distraught as she approached, and although we were caught off guard by the question, we began by acknowledging the veracity of her situation. People often use their gifts in pursuit of a purpose that is not only helpful to others, but a lifeline for others. Particularly in the case of underfunded and understaffed agencies and departments, these individuals are gently pressed to do more and offer more of their precious gifts. And often, the very gift that makes them such a lifesaver for others (i.e., their compassion), is the gift that leads them to accept more work and eventually compromise their sense of balance.

Throughout this book, we have deliberately used the word "gifts" rather than "gift." We are multidimensional creatures, with a variety of talents and skills, each of which is clamoring to see the light of day. The zealous use of one gift in and of itself is not problematic; however, the disregard of other, important gifts and the failure to "become" can be the culprit of imbalance.

As we probed further, this resonated with the administrator as a reasonable explanation for what was happening. Many of her counselors had families who were not being nurtured. They had artistic and creative pursuits that were not tended to. They had senses of humor that often were buried under tales of tragedy and desperation. In short, their over-expression of compassion for others led to the under-expression of other gifts.

We also explored the idea of roadblocks to becoming. Did her counselors have the chance to discover new and unpolished gifts? Were they growing in their positions, or were they utilizing the same skills over and over again? She thought about it, and relayed that this was the case for some of her more seasoned counselors. One came to mind for her, a young man who was passionate about advocacy and lobbying when he first arrived five years previous. As his case load was increased and he dealt with tougher and tougher cases, he became entrenched and no longer spoke of the difference that he could make at the state level. She resolved to encourage him to reengage this gift and purpose, even with his current case load, to determine if it produced meaning for him.

Ironically, this may be the most reasonable use of the term "balance" in the work-life balance realm. Balance does not refer to balancing time, energy, or schedules; rather, it involves balancing the expression of gifts to ensure that all are engaged and that each facet of purpose is attended.

NOTES

1. Stewart D. Friedman and Jeffrey H. Greenhaus, *Work and Family—Allies or Enemies? What Happens When Business Professionals Confront Life Choices* (Oxford: Oxford University Press, 2000).

2. Joan Kofodimos, *Balancing Act: How Managers Can Integrate Successful Careers and Fulfilling Personal Lives* (San Francisco: Jossey-Bass, 1993), 84.

3. Robert C. Fuller, *Religion and the Life Cycle* (Philadelphia: Fortress Press, 1988), 63.

4. Fuller, *Religion and the Life Cycle*, 69.

5. Harold S. Kushner, *Living a Life that Matters* (New York: Anchor Books, 2001), 61–65.

6. Thomas Merton, *New Seeds of Contemplation* (New York: New Directions Books, 1961), 14.

7. The Gallup organization has produced intriguing ideas on the nature and impact of engagement. They have concluded that when employees are not engaged in their work, they are more likely to express discontent in their lives in general. For example, see Steve Crabtree, "Bringing Work Problems Home," *Gallup Management Journal* (June, 2003) http://gmj.gallup.com/gmj_surveys/articles.asp?i=350 (18 June 2003).

8. A well used metaphor drawn from Spinoza's *Ethics Geometrically Demonstrated*. For a wonderful (and admittedly simplified) look at this example, see Jostein Gaardner, *Sophie's World: A Novel About the History of Philosophy* (New York: Brkley Books, 1996), 253–55.

9. James M. Kouzes and Barry Z. Posner, *The Leadership Challenge*, 3rd ed. (San Francisco: Jossey-Bass, 2002), 52.

10. Victor E. Frankl, *Man's Search for Meaning* (New York: Touchstone, 1984), 113.

11. Thomas Merton, *No Man Is An Island* (New York: Barnes & Noble Books, 1983), 117.

12. For example, see James C. Quick and Jonathan D. Quick, *Organizational Stress and Preventive Management* (New York: McGraw-Hill, 1984), 23–24. An interesting discussion of this phenomenon is offered by Mihalyi Csikszentmilalyi, *Finding Flow: The Psychology of Engagement with Everyday Life* (New York: Basic Books, 1997).

13. Quick and Quick, *Organizational Stress and Preventive Management*, 43–74.

14. This theme is increasingly being stressed in leadership and executive development programs. See John H. Zenger and Joseph Folkman, *The Extraordinary Leader: Turning Good Managers into Great Leaders* (New York: McGraw-Hill, 2002); and Marcus Buckingham and Donald O. Clifton, *Now Discover Your Strengths: How to Develop Your Talents and Those of the People You Manage* (New York: Simon & Schuster Adult Publishing Group, 2001).

15. David Whyte, *Crossing the Unknown Sea: Work as a Pilgrimage of Identity* (New York: Riverhead Books, 2001), 132.

Chapter Seven

Balancing

At this point, you have an understanding of the core self. After working through the exercises in the previous chapter, you also have at least an initial understanding of *your own* core self—those gifts that make you who you are, the purpose you feel called to serve, and your search for both being and becoming. This understanding, as we've discussed, will deepen over time and will evolve as life experience and further reflection launch you to even higher expressions of gifts and purpose. This knowledge alone can help you feel a greater sense of balance. On the Greek god Apollo's oracle of Delphi is the inscription, "Know Thyself", which meant much more to the Greeks than basic self-understanding. It more fully meant to be complete, whole, and to live out the potential of who you are as an individual.[1] Our hope is that you now know yourself better and have a richer picture of your core self.

This richer understanding is likely exhilarating in a way that only comes from discovering some veritable truth - that euphoric "got it," reminiscent of finding a solution to the pesky "two trains leaving their stations at the same time" story problem that haunted you long ago in physics class. Exhilaration is energy, and in this chapter we will help you direct that energy into the creation of a life in balance. In short, you are now at the point where reflection gives way to action and ideation becomes reality.

We've given this point of inflection of very specific name. It is aptly called, "balancing." Balancing is action taken in service of aligning one's gifts and purpose with one's life situation. It is an ongoing process of creating that dynamic equilibrium that produces feelings of balance. Understand that the use of the term "dynamic" is purposeful. Our equilibrium point is not static; it is a moving target that involves constant adjustment as the various priorities shift in their relevance. Rather than viewing balance as the point at which both ends of the scale are equally weighted (a state that is conceivably static), we view balance as the action taken to move a gymnast from one end of the balance beam to the other. She is in constant motion, action and correction, adjustment and readjustment, even when she appears to be standing still. Each action, no matter how small, provides both feedback as to the wisdom of the action (through feelings of balance and fulfillment or imbalance and wanting) and information as to which action should be taken next. But, we are ahead of ourselves here. First, we must address the fundamental balance dilemma.

THE FUNDAMENTAL BALANCE DILEMMA

Cognizant of your core self, you are now armed with a fresh and empowering awareness. You have embarked on a critical philosophic and reflective journey. Now, we must return to the reality that surrounds you day-in and day-out. Important as reflective journeys are to our overall psychological health, reflection must be translated into pragmatic existence. In essence, we all must ask, "How does my sense of self, my core, my gifts, and my purpose coincide with the situations and demands faced while living life?" In thinking through this question, you will encounter a central point of inner-conflict, a conflict that we refer to as the fundamental balance dilemma.

The fundamental balance dilemma exists when we recognize that the demands of our current situations conflict with our core selves. As in any dilemma, each option produces some level of undesirable outcome. On one hand, if we succumb to the demands of the situation, we risk losing our core self in the process. On the other hand, if we affirm and move in accordance with our core self, situations and environments must be adjusted, extracting the costs of time, energy, power, prestige, and comfort.

There is no escape for the serious reader, only options. How can the dilemma be addressed and resolved? Most simply, one can deny and sublimate the core self. We have already addressed the myriad reasons and ways this occurs. Further, most of the people in our studies have already tried this, with consistently unsatisfying results. While this approach may provide a temporary release of tension, it cannot be the route to ultimate balance and meaning. A sacrificed core self will eventually feel thwarted, belittled, and minimized, leaving one to either bask in resentment or vacillate in the cauldron of meaninglessness. We assume you have been here and want out.

So we must turn to our conditions, our situations, the environments in which we live and work. How can these environments be viewed, structured, adjusted, or changed to allow the creative expression of the gifts and purpose that ultimately birth the experience of balance and meaning? What are those practical adjustments that foster expressions of our core selves? The answers differ, as all core selves are unique and different. Yet, certain fundamental themes must be noted, and that is the purpose of this chapter.

PERMISSION

Our first responsibility in a chapter devoted to helping you create an environment that supports and encourages your gifts and purpose is empowering you to do so. As an initial (albeit whimsical) exercise, transport yourself back to seventh grade. You need to be excused from school. Your mother writes you a permission slip, which begins, "Please excuse my son (or daughter) from school at 1:15 because . . ." She signs the permission slip, and you are then not only allowed, but expected to leave school for the dentist appointment or other engagement.

It is now time for another permission slip, one that releases you to make the changes necessary to align your purpose and gifts. "Please allow [insert your name here] to examine and make necessary changes to his or her life because . . ." Fill in the permission slip with what has brought you here. Perhaps your permission slip will read: "because she feels as if she is meant for something more in this life," or "because the active involvement in the growth and development of his children is part of his life's purpose that is not being acknowledged." Or, maybe:" because he is experiencing symptoms of depression and lack of enthusiasm about life." We will happily sign your permission slip, whatever your reasoning. You no longer need to pretend as if the life you have created is the life that will bring you balance if you would just try harder.

Although seemingly unsophisticated, the exercise is an important one. All levity aside, many of us feel trapped in our current life situations, many of which do not afford us the circumstances that allow us to use our gifts and realize our purpose. This feeling of ensnarement is likely heightened by the fact that you now know what some of your gifts are, and you likely have at least a cursory understanding of your purpose. The urge to act, to make changes, is natural, and it is what we are counting on as we channel your urges in an appropriate and meaning-producing way. However, there is likely also a force holding you back from making changes, a force that carries with it subtle emotions of shame and ignorance. Left unchecked, this force can stall your efforts and inhibit real change.

This restraining force is also natural. When looking around for the party responsible for your current life situation, the situation that is not producing the feelings of meaning and balance you seek, there is only one person holding the bag . . . you. While we've discussed the influences that may have steered you wrong, ultimately you made the choices that have led you here. If you are not happy with your situation, you may be feeling ashamed that you made the "wrong" choices. If you are discovering new information about gifts and purpose that you did not previously possess, you may be feeling ignorant and incompetent. Neither emotion is particularly affirming, and neither emotion squares well with the confidence needed to make meaningful life changes.

We encourage you not to suppress these emotions, as they are real and expected given what you may be facing. Rather, we encourage you to reframe them, evoking a different perspective that is functional and moves you forward rather than keeps you stuck. First, recognize (as we have already discussed) that there is no wasted experience. The life situation that you have created has given you important data to help you determine what is not meaningful, what is not at your core. Secondly, realize that if your choices got you here, your choices can also get you where you need to be to create a life of meaning and balance. Too often, we become paralyzed at this point, rationalizing that "we made our bed, now we have to lie in it." While not completely false—we do have some roles and responsibilities that are non-negotiable—it is also incomplete. Each of us has the power to move toward authenticity and full expression of core self. More than that, it is what we must do if we are to experience meaning. Scott Peck offers that "to be free people we must assume total responsibility for ourselves, but in doing so we must possess the capacity to reject responsibility that is not truly ours."[2]

Let us first turn to those "non-negotiables." These fall into two categories. First are the physical, mental, and spiritual boundaries in which our life unfolds. We cannot attend to our gifts and purpose unless we are physically healthy, mentally stable, and spiritually fulfilled. Second are the value boundaries, those aspects of our lives so fundamental to who we are that anything we do in service of balancing must not disturb these critical roles and responsibilities.

PHYSICAL, MENTAL, AND SPIRITUAL FOUNDATION

Up to now, our approach has been expansive, encouraging you to think openly, reflectively and creatively about your personal balance equation. We also suggested that care be taken to avoid being unduly driven by the community of expectations and mixed messages that barrage our lives. To a large extent, we have worked to remove impositions and boundaries, not to place more in your path.

This section is a bit different. It draws on some of the best available research we have to suggest additional boundaries within which most of us must work to create our own personal balance. While we continue to be cautious about the unnecessarily restrictive nature of hard and fast rules (as each of us is remarkably unique), there are certain boundaries or parameters of action that serve as important guidelines in our ongoing movements for life balance.

We can consider these foundational boundaries as falling into three categories, although these are neither discrete nor mutually exclusive: physical, mental, and spiritual. If these foundations are neglected or minimized, we will not have the energy to exercise our gifts, fulfill our potential, or experience our full sense of meaning. Let's discuss these demands in more detail.

Physical Foundations

Research abounds as to the importance of a healthy diet and exercise. We believe these are important aspects of your physical foundation to which you must attend. Your physicians, personal trainers, and others all provide you advice and support in this arena. We have no desire to add to the advice of these professionals, as our expertise lies elsewhere. We will simply say that these foundations are important and must receive some basic level of attention before you can obtain the balance you seek. We do wish to touch on one physical foundation, though. It is a foundation that gets little attention but is also a pressing issue for today's executives and professionals on the path to balance. It is the physical foundation of sleep.

We have worked with Dave, the CEO of a mid-sized business, for nearly ten years. In all that time, Dave has confided to us that he sleeps about 4 1/2 hours each night and rarely if ever exceeds 5 hours of sleep. Despite this extended pattern, he appears to remain healthy and productive. He has a wonderful family and a highly selective social life. He rises at 4:00 A.M. each day, reads and does daily devotionals, works out three days a week, and is at the office for a thirteen-hour day that begins at 6 am. He is absolutely convinced that his business requires such dedication. Is there a problem here?

Established and well-accepted research becomes our guide. Most evidence indicates, quite convincingly, that we need about 7 hours of sleep each night.[3] In fact, the acceptable range of sleep is fairly narrow, generally from 6 to 8 hours a night. While there may be slight variations depending on age or other temporary physical or emotional considerations, getting less than this prescribed amount is seen as risky and more than the prescribed amount is probably unnecessary. (We are careful to recognize that we are speaking of "good" hours of sleep, not those hours disrupted by some element of sleep disturbance or difficulty. In general, if you sleep 7 hours a night and still wake up feeling tired, some type of sleep disturbance [such as sleep apnea] may be the culprit).

So what is the message here for hard-chargers like Dave? It is matter of vulnerability. Dave is placing himself in a realm that may be unhealthy over the long-run. Dave is not feeling elements of imbalance at this point; rather, his sense is one of fulfillment and balance. However, he is engaged in risky behavior and we would simply raise the cautionary flag. It becomes important for Dave to consider some honest and objective self-appraisal of the boundary violations that may eventually lead to imbalance.

Intriguingly, the research that supports the importance of attending to the totality of one's physical foundation comes from studies in which the optimal number of work hours was the focus of study. While interesting findings in and of themselves, what this research says to us, loud and clear, is that work becomes debilitating when it encroaches upon these physical foundations. The negative results of working too much are almost always physical and psychological; rarely do we find that workaholics encounter career disaster directly. However, they may find themselves face to face with a debilitating physical ailment that indirectly sabotages their career success. Let's look at this research before moving forward.

We used an array of data in Chapter 2 to build the case that many of us are working more and enjoying it less. Should we work less? A knee-jerk response would be to say yes, and that response has merit. Years of research (as well as practical experience) tells us that long work hours are associated with increased stress levels. And, the manifestations of that stress appear rather striking. Considerable research evidence has noted a link between hours of work and ill health.[4] In short, there is consistent support that work overload is the strongest single variable affecting work exhaustion or burnout.

Consequently, a pertinent question moves to center stage. Just what constitutes too much work? Researchers have attempted to offer specifics. In a classic study of workers in California, Buell and Breslow reported that men who worked more than 48 hours a week had twice the incidence of coronary heart disease than their counterparts who worked less than 48 hours a week.[5] Harrington, after an extensive literature review, asserted that working in excess of 48–56 hours a week was harmful.[6] Barton and Folkard found a similar outcome among shift workers, noting that those working 48 hours a week or more manifested higher levels of mental health (anxiety and neuroticism) and physical health problems (cardiovascular and digestive) when compared with those working fewer hours.[7] Complicating the picture even more is strong evidence suggesting that long working hours are frequently associated with corollary behaviors that may exacerbate underlying health concerns. These behaviors include the tendency to smoke more, eat less nutritiously, and exhibit less healthy sleeping habits as working hours increase.[8]

With due respect to those of you whose typical work week extends far beyond the 50-hour mark, the red flags of imbalance should be going up based upon the research we've discussed. We cannot assert with certainty that exceeding the 50-hour mark will produce debilitating outcomes. But we can say this: Exceeding the 50-hour parameter for an extended period of time renders one vulnerable to a range of physical and psychological fallout that cannot be taken lightly. The data is simply too consistent and too convincing to believe otherwise.

Mental Foundations

By way of introducing this foundation, consider the following metaphor. Most plant managers understand that running a machine at full capacity, 24/7, leads to malfunction, disrepair, ultimately lost efficiency and productivity, and an increased error rate. We're better off periodically taking the machine down, moving it off-line, and allowing the necessary remediation and preventative reparations to take place. The same is true for the human machine.

We've worked with many talented professionals who are utilizing their gifts and reaching toward core purpose through their engagement in roles and responsibilities. They've allowed themselves the freedom to stretch, take on new responsibilities that synchronize their gifts with their life situation. This is exactly what we advocate. We applaud them. Yet, often these professionals smile at us through the bleary eyes of fatigue, the slumped posture of near exhaustion. There seems to be no rest in their "life of balance." Accordingly, is it really a life in balance? Or, is it again a life facing the vulnerability of stepping beyond the sense of meaning to a sense of overwhelmed activity?

As with the machine described above, we cannot run at full capacity. Even when we do nothing but that which we are meant to do (i.e., operating from our core), there is a mental, psychological, and emotional limit to our abundance. As we discover, celebrate, and draw into our lives situations that capitalize on our gifts, we may find it easy to find engagement and balance in so many activities that we are metaphorically at 100% capacity. The human machine runs most optimally when it is allowed down time to renew and replenish.

Many writers have suggested that people need downtime within their week in order to maintain healthy balance.[9] We agree but offer a reframe on what downtime looks like. We suggest downtime is time away from your typical routine. It need not be a period of inactivity, which may be particularly frustrating and boring for some people. Rather, a break in pattern is necessary in order to create a sense of renewal. A hike in the woods may be down time, as may be lunch with a friend, shooting baskets with your son, or just curling up with a good book. If you normally dash out of your house in the morning with a cup of coffee and the newspaper under your arm, perhaps down time is sharing breakfast with your spouse at a local café. At any rate, down time is needed in order to maintain the mental foundation that is your springboard to a life in balance.

Spiritual Foundations

Any in-depth look at core self, balance, and ultimate meaning must address the spiritual dimension of our existence. We are decidedly spiritual, and most people identify themselves as spiritual beings. A 2005 survey of over 1000 Americans found that 84 % of the respondents felt that spirituality was important in their lives, with nearly 6 of 10 indicating that it was "very important."[10] Even in an age when fewer people profess and practice involvement in traditional organized religions, more and more people believe that there is some power greater than them, some power that extends beyond their personal sense of understanding and control. Scholars argue that although nearly 40% of Americans have no connection with a formal religion, nine out of ten believe in a Higher Power, and nearly all claim to be strongly spiritual at a personal level.[11] One can logically conclude that contemporary America is more spiritual even while being less religious. There is no denying, and certainly no excusing, that the particular conception of balance that we have offered is one of intense spirituality.

But, what is spirituality? What does this strange, experiential, and essentially idiosyncratic concept really mean? The literal definition of spirit means to breathe or to breathe life into or to be filled with the breath of life.[12] As such, spirituality implies that one embodies the spirit of life itself. Ashforth and Pratt have suggested that spirituality, as an individual experience, consists of three core dimensions: transcendence, holism, and harmony.[13] In this context, transcendence refers to a transcendence of self, suggesting that one is connected to purposes and meanings larger than themselves. Most of us spend our days focused on concerns of immediacy—paying the bills, advancing our career, sending the kids to college. Transcendence focuses on existence itself. Of course, such a perspective emphasizes a sense of the meaning of existence, which is typically structured through one's belief in a Higher Power (although the name and nature of that Power may vary considerably). Transcendence occurs as one rises beyond all roles and expectations to live and be the spirit of the Higher Power.

Further, spirituality allows one to more carefully and fully discover the potential of his or her core self in such a way that the various domains, arenas, and roles of life connect in an integrative way that allows one's potential to be expansive or transcendent. Accordingly, for many people, spirituality becomes an anchor, as important (or perhaps preeminent) as physical and emotional health. Here, spirituality serves as a filter for providing perspective on how roles and demands are understood and addressed. Listen to the straightforward words of one respondent who explained his search for balance:

> "There is one anchoring unit. For me it is spiritual balance. This makes everything else make sense. It defines what the other parts look like. It is the lens for looking at all other parts."

It is important to offer some related comments. By emphasizing spiritual-ity, we are neither dismissing nor minimizing the role of religion. Instead, we argue that religion may play a key role, serving as a vehicle for promoting and encouraging one's personal spirituality. Religion offers many positive out-comes for its holder, including physical and emotional outcomes. Argyle has noted, "We know that stress impairs the immune system and that positive mood and close relations enhance it. Religion would be expected to benefit the immune system through these different aspects of peace of mind and re-duced stress, the relation with God and the positive moods induced by church services."[14] The data seems to offer support. For example, most surveys pres-ent a clear but relatively weak effect of religion on happiness[15], and a meta-analysis of 56 American surveys found a positive but modest correlation (.16) between religion and well-being.[16]

In sum, whether one explicitly realizes it or not, the search for gifts (and even more specifically the search for purpose) is a spiritual exercise. Rarely does one's exploration of purpose fail to extend beyond an egocentric focus. Commonly, one's purpose reaches out to others and acknowledges a personal transcendence. Further, the evolutionary and expansive nature of our core self presents elements of potentiality and creativity that are part of the dynamic essence of spirituality.

The physical, mental and spiritual boundaries are fundamental to creating a life in balance. They are, in fact, essential to human life. While we have some choice as to how these needs are satisfied, they must be satisfied to some basic level. To ignore these boundaries is risky at best, and at worst, to do so sabo-tages any attempts at a life of meaning. In the next section, we discuss value boundaries that further define the playing field in which you will create your life in balance. Unlike physical, mental, and spiritual boundaries, the presence and magnitude of these boundaries varies considerably from person to person. Yet, like physical, mental, and spiritual boundaries, respecting value boundaries is also necessary if one's efforts at balancing are to be successful. Accordingly, physical, mental, spiritual and value boundaries must be fervently protected.

VALUE BOUNDARIES

Remember that it is our view that maximizing the expression of gifts while fulfilling your life's purpose is the means to a life of balance and meaning. It follows that the actions taken to balance one's life involve decisions that lead to expressing more of the core self. It is the goal that all gifts and all aspects of purpose are addressed through one's roles and responsibilities, and that each role and responsibility taps at least one gift, although the more of the core self that each role taps, the better.

Before you begin to take inventory and eventual action, which may involve some fairly significant shifts in your life situation, it is important to touch base with one additional piece—your value boundaries. These value boundaries are the underlying, personal set of ideals that must not be compromised if one is to experience a life of meaning and balance. There is no formula and there is no way we can prescribe what these can or should be. Value boundaries are decidedly personal, and they may include family, travel, autonomy, or frankly, any ideal you would use to complete the sentence, "In order to live a life of meaning, I will not sacrifice. . . ."

Let's explore the idea of value boundaries in practice. Recently, we worked with a young entrepreneur who was considering a major change in his career. Not surprisingly, the prospect of change followed closely on the heels of a deeply personal spiritual experience and his return to his "spiritual roots." Our discussion was taking place to help him sort through his career options.

We began with the standard question, "What do you really want to do?" He commented that although he had given that very question considerable thought, he was really unsure. Fair enough, and not that unusual. So a follow-up was needed. "What parameters do you place around your decision? What elements absolutely must be included in this new career?" His response was immediate, obvious evidence of thoughtful reflection. "First, the job cannot take me away from the family the way my previous jobs have done—seventy-five hours left little for my family. I cannot and will not do that again. Second, I have been a pretty hardnosed businessman. I've burned some bridges. There are people who don't like me." With a few probes, it became obvious that he had been a ruthless, win-at-all-costs leader. He vowed that he could not continue to treat people in this way. He was committed to dealing with people in an open, trusting, and above-board manner.

Although the term was never used, he had identified two important value boundaries—parameters that must be present as he moved forward. These boundaries are the minimal absolutes that must be ingrained in his decision. These boundaries were concern for family and concern for people. These boundaries became meaningful benchmarks as he considered career options.

TAKING INVENTORY

At this point, it is time to look at your life situation through the lens of your core self. By "life situation," we mean the constellation of roles and responsibilities in one's life at any given point in time. For instance, I am the owner of my own business, a life coach and counselor, and a yoga teacher, not to mention a family member, friend, and life partner. But, my roles and responsibilities are richer than can be captured by labels. My business is new, providing opportunities for creativity, vision, and variety. It also brings with it a need to establish my own schedule and manage cash flow, activities that I have not engaged in throughout my short career. My business role is professional, but also helpful. My role as a counselor and yoga teacher is also one of helpfulness, but in a very different capacity. We don't speak of the bottom line, we speak of emotional and cognitive health and growth. Here, I have responsibilities for the safety of my clients and students, and a commitment to serve a healing role in the lives of others. Each role and responsibility either taps my gifts or calls me to develop them, and each role and responsibility will change over time. While my role as counselor will be with me for the foreseeable future, the context it provides and the opportunities it presents for the expression of my core self will change as I move from new therapist to seasoned mental health professional. Acknowledging that all roles and responsibilities have some degree of fluidity, one's life situation can be seen as a snapshot of the context in which the core self can be expressed.

While it is likely you have been looking at the snapshot to some extent, the core self has been largely unrecognized in an explicit way, which means your assessment may have been unduly clouded by mixed messages and patterns. As a colleague put it, we often "live by the rules of that which we've forgotten," or we persist in ways of managing our time and our relationships that were logical and reasonable for a past situation but which have no bearing on our present reality.[17] It is time to begin the process of realigning our "rules" in order to create a synchronous, meaning-producing life situation.

As a first step, we invite you to simply list the roles and responsibilities that comprise your life situation. Be sure to capture the richness of these roles. You may be a daughter, but that role is influenced by the geographic proximity of your parents, their health, and the ways in which they wish to be a part of your life. While it may become apparent in this process how your roles either do or do not allow for the expression of your core self, this is not our initial focus. Save those thoughts, but do not allow them to detract from your inventory of your life situation.

Once your roles and responsibilities are laid out in front of you, you may be aware of several things. The first reaction is often a reaction to the quantity. We are often unaware of how many important roles we fill, and we are often unaware of the nuances that make them unique and different from the experiences of others. Your second reaction will likely reveal itself when you take the next step, which is to evaluate each of your roles and responsibilities against your core self and purpose.

It will not surprise you that there is no one magical formula for doing so. In a twist of thinking, the most appropriate way for you to evaluate your life situation against your gifts is to use your gifts. For instance, if one of your gifts is structure and preparation, creating the matrix we present for illustration may be an effective approach. If you have a gift of intuition and "trusting your gut," you will have no patience for a matrix. Rather, simply bringing your core self to "top-of-mind awareness" regularly will be enough to carry out the needed evaluation. If you are highly relational, you may want to carry out the exercise with a friend or significant other. Our approach will be to make the process as concrete and tangible as possible; however, we would be remiss and utterly contradictory if we asked you to follow our formulaic approach in blatant disregard for what you know will work best for you.

THE MATRIX APPROACH

One way to look at your roles in a way that allows you to see their impact upon your sense of balance and meaning is to create a simple matrix. This approach allows you to evaluate your roles and responsibilities as they relate to your life's purpose and your gifts, the ultimate criteria when it comes to creating a life of meaning. Begin by listing your gifts and purpose down the left hand side of your notebook, journal, or spreadsheet. List your roles and responsibilities across the top. Then, for each role, place a mark in the row if the role taps into that particular gift or purpose.

	Role 1	Role 2	. . .	Role 12
Purpose 1				
Purpose 2				
Gift 1				
Gift 2				
. . .				
Gift 8				

We encourage you to devise a system that works for you. You may place an "x" in the column if that role fully taps a gift, but a "√" if it only partially does so. You may also know that in the near future, one of your roles will no longer serve the purpose it once did; this scenario may involve some other notation. Try to carry out the entire process of evaluation with some degree of objectivity and equanimity. Emotions and concerns will undoubtedly surface. While we encourage you to acknowledge them and perhaps even stop the process to consider them deeply, do not allow them to guide any decision-making until you have had time to view the entire picture of your roles and responsibilities. Also, following such an introspective exercise, we recommend avoiding action for a period of time to allow your discoveries to sink in. There will be plenty of time to take action and adjust to any findings that trouble you.

As the entire picture unfolds, realize that even with a process as structured as the matrix, there are some higher level, unquantifiable considerations to be made. It is important to realize that the contributions that one role makes in terms of maximizing the expression of your core self cannot be considered in a vacuum. It is the constellation of roles, the life situation, that produces maximum meaning. At this point, an example may be helpful. When I was in graduate school, I valued my role as a mentor and advisor to more junior students. Not only did I help them with the technical aspects of research and consulting project design, I was also a confidant and a source of emotional and psychological support. As I was finishing my dissertation, I was forced to move out of this role. It was time for others to "take the reigns" and many of my project management responsibilities had been transferred to others. My gifts of support and my purpose to facilitate growth and development of others did not have an outlet, and I was met with a void in this area of my life. In order to fill that void, I joined the Big Brothers/Big Sisters program, and for several hours each week, these gifts had a new context in which to be expressed.

When I took my first faculty position in a different state. I also resumed my Big Sister role in my new location. I had such a fantastic experience in graduate school that it was a "no brainer" to resume this volunteer activity. What I did not consider is that my role as faculty member also served my gifts of support and connectedness; I advised several students academically, and the occasional tearful student tugged at my gifts of psychological support. My role as a Big Sister had become redundant, even though it was serving the same gifts it always had. Moreover, my desires to write creatively were not being exercised, in part due to the time constraints of this redundant role. It is important to view the entire landscape of your life situation and ask yourself: Are each of my gifts being served in some way? Are there gifts that are not being served? Are there roles that are redundant? Are there roles that are serving few if any gifts?

It is also important to realize that roles cannot be evaluated completely objectively. Resist the urge to look at your matrix as a scorecard in which all tic marks are weighted equally. One role as committee member may not tap many of your gifts, but it allows you to express your gift of strategic thinking in a way that other roles in life do not. Particularly if your membership does not take time away from underutilized gifts, we would suggest this role be kept and nurtured. Another role may tap many gifts, but may be redundant, as in the example above. Yet another role may be a grand experiment. The painting class you took last year allowed you to explore and learn a new area, but you may find you have neither the talent nor the passion to create such pieces of art.

Balancing

Armed with your foundational boundaries (i.e., physical, mental, and spiritual needs), your value boundaries, and your inventory of your life situation as viewed through your core self, it is time to engage in balancing. Foundational and value boundaries serve as the demarcations for the arena in which you will create balance. Similar to "playing in bounds" on a sports field, you will utilize all possibilities within these boundaries while not subjecting yourself to the penalties just outside the white lines. Once these boundaries are established, real decision-making can begin.

For example, we interviewed a successful entrepreneur who described her philosophy of core self and balance. Obviously dedicated to her business and family, her stature in the business community led to constant requests for community activities and outreach. How does she decide among all the opportunities placed before her? At her core, she admitted that community enhancement and people connectivity were a key part of her purpose. Accordingly, she fine-tuned her community perspectives to zero in on those areas where her gifts of communication and creativity could most uniquely contribute. She participates in school and education-related causes, but turns down most requests that fall outside these bounds. She is using her gifts and purpose to guide the creation of her life's work. She is making those decisions with an awareness of her core self as a guiding mechanism. Her value boundaries, and to some extent her core self, limit her choices, but also assure that any choice she makes within those limits has the potential to bring her balance.

Further, she understands that each decision and each activity brings new challenges, yet also new growth, new potential, and a new becoming. Interestingly, she noted that one of her challenges was to leave enough time for herself. Aware of this priority, she makes it a point to tune in to "her own conversation" as much as she does that of others. Whether while walking in the morning or taking quiet time, she reflects upon who she is becoming and enjoys the adventure that unfolds before her. By tuning into her own conversation, her gifts and values are always at the forefront of all the messages guiding her choices.

For ease of explanation, we suggest actions you will take can be grouped into four categories. It will be helpful to discuss the types of actions you may take before encouraging you to do so. To help you visualize our direction, consider the following diagram:

	Core Self Activated	**Core Self Not Activated**
Current Roles	Embrace and Nuture	Withdraw and Release
Future Roles	Select and Add	Monitor Potential and Opportunity

On the vertical are the current roles in your life situation. On the horizontal, find the degree to which the core self is actualized. Consider the upper left hand quadrant. This quadrant represents current roles in which you are engaged that tap your gifts and purpose. In essence, these are the roles that activate your core self. Logically, this quadrant must be embraced and nurtured. You may find several of your value absolutes reside here. That process of embracing and nurturing begins with recognizing the significance and necessity of the roles that reside here. Once recognized, it is important to unapologetically make time for these roles, and to be completely present and attentive while fulfilling them. If you have been with us through the process of paying attention to the emotions, thoughts, and reactions that arise throughout your day, you will have noted that wholeheartedly fulfilling these roles provoke not only positive reactions, but feelings of meaning and balance. It is only through the demands of our busy lives and our unwillingness to explore deeply the connections between our roles, responsibilities, gifts and purpose that our commitment to these roles has become compromised. It is through the acquisition of some bad habits that it is no longer natural to spend time and energy here.

Next, consider the upper right hand quadrant. Here you will find roles and responsibilities that demand your time, commitment, and energy, but which do not tap the gifts and purpose at your core. Many people are surprised to find at least one of these roles lurking in the folds of their life situations, draining personal resources but offering little in return. Interestingly, such roles can become common, assumed, and even habitual because we have not acknowledged the illusory nature of the payoff. It is easy to assume that expending time, energy, and resources buys us meaningful outcomes. In this case, it does not. It buys us frustration and depleted enthusiasm because we are not acting from our core. These roles may include committees or other volunteer activities; other times these may be your role as a friend to someone with whom you no longer have common interests. Tough as it may be, you must selectively relinquish these roles and responsibilities if you are to achieve meaning and balance. Even though these roles must be released, your withdrawal often involves difficult conversations with others, a topic we will cover in the next chapter. Your withdrawal from these roles may also seem unusual or uncomfortable to you as you are modifying an ingrained behavioral pattern. There is comfort and security in our patterns. Again, the fallout of relinquishment will be discussed further in the next chapter.

Next, consider the lower left-hand quadrant, what we are calling "the additive" quadrant. Let us warn you up front that our message here is somewhat counter-intuitive and often surprises our audiences initially. To them (and probably you), balance is not about adding anything; it is about taking away, giving one room to breathe, slowing down. But unquestionably, the additive component is central to our focus on gifts, purpose, and an expansion of one's core self. The additive approach involves selectively and judiciously incorporating new or expanded roles and responsibilities that help you make the most of your underutilized talents more fully. In the short term, you may experience a life that is fuller, but perhaps also more harried. Understandably, this is why so many people shy away from addressing this quadrant. We hope that you will muster the courage to do so, as the uncomfortable state of affairs is temporary. More importantly, the meaning engendered by your pursuit of these new roles provides you the additional fuel needed to manage your increased responsibilities. Stated in different terms, these core-engaging roles and responsibilities will deliver an unexpected shot of meaning and fulfillment that will provide the fuel needed to grasp and thrive within the new constellation of demands.

The additive quadrant always reminds us of our friend Tom. Energetic and enthusiastic, Tom's boyish smile and sincere charm cut an impressive social picture. Tom is a savvy businessman, runs his own consulting company, and serves as a coach and confidant to an array of business leaders. He is a popular and much sought after speaker.

But, in order to fully understand and appreciate Tom, we must mention his battle with spasmodic torticollis. This relatively rare neurological disease affects Tom's muscle movements, causes him significant pain, and restricts the scope of his activity. However, you'll never hear Tom complain. Instead he uses his condition as a focal point in his speeches. He is a believer in the old adage that it's not the hand you're dealt, but how you play that hand that really counts. And Tom plays his hand for all it's worth. Rather than waste time in self pity, Tom has chosen to take his condition as a challenge and use his plight as a way to reach others and build them up. Tom is richly aware of his gifts and he pushes himself as far as he physically can. Rather than back away from speaking requests or coaching opportunities, he cherishes each opportunity to share his message and as long as he is physically able, he'll add as much to his plate as possible. While his work is physically exhausting given his disease, his works allows him tap his rich gifts, thereby providing him energy and satisfaction that keeps him going day after day. It is important to note that Tom does not achieve his sense of meaning by indiscriminately agreeing to requests. Rather, Tom is selective in what he does. He accepts only those invitations for which he feels a deep sense of resonance at his core.

It is easy to dismiss the last quadrant. It includes roles we neither occupy nor gravitate toward if our current gifts and purpose are engaged. However, this is a quadrant that encapsulates potential, a quadrant that embodies opportunity. Since our core is always moving and evolving, we must be open to new roles that will allow us to experience new growth. Some forays into this arena will be false starts. Others will be vehicles for finding new meaning. This is the quadrant that ensures that you continue to create balance and meaning in your life beyond your current circumstances. With regard to this quadrant, your task is simple, almost so simple it may fall off your radar screen. Monitor. Monitor both your internal and external worlds. Watch for surfacing gifts that need a context in which to be expressed. Take note of opportunities to fulfill roles that may enhance your gifts and engage your purpose more profoundly. Hold these as potentialities that, once activated, move into the realm of the additive approach.

Consider the case of Anthony. Anthony is a mid-level manager for a large service organization. He also teaches part-time at a local university. He is a voracious reader. He communicates well and he is a powerful writer. He inspires and engages those around him. These are his gifts, enhanced and polished through his experiences and life situation. Anthony, at times somewhat jokingly, hints at "the book I'm going to write." In fact, he recognizes that the book is within him and it will be a rich expression of his experiences and insights. He understands that "the book" will be a further expression of his unique talents. In short, he is monitoring his evolving core self. But, Anthony is also monitoring his life situation. He is watchful of his changing roles and responsibilities as a manager, father, and teacher, and how they will evolve to allow the context in which this gift may be expressed. At some point, his evolving gifts and life situation will mesh, and he will find the right mix of time, energy, and passion to manifest his budding gift.

EASY, RIGHT? WRONG.

We understand the complex difficulties in making choices. All too often, we trust that others know better what's best for us than we do. We agree to the assignment or the promotion, even when we know, deep down, that it does not align with our core self. Perhaps this is because we know how often we have let ourselves down, how often we have not pursued what is at our core in favor of the desires and expectations of others. Making the first decision from the core can be terrifying, but over time, as your gifts and purpose become more salient and you begin to reap the benefits from acting in this way, it will become second nature to defer to your life purpose. And you will do so without apology or regret.

We presented four types of actions, four ways to engage in balancing, or action taken in service of aligning one's core self with one's life situation. Conceptually, it is straightforward and easy to understand, but as you begin this process there are three stumbling blocks that deserve mention.

Evolution

This task of balancing is problematic because life situations do *change* and core selves do *evolve*. We addressed this to some extent in our fourth quadrant above, but we must continue this discussion briefly here because we realize that some people have great difficulty in recognizing the ways their situations change and the ways their core shifts and grows.

In some respects, it is difficult to realize why this dimension is so difficult for our audiences to handle. Business people are trained to view the world as an open system, always changing. We further recognize that any business that refuses to confront this reality will fail. It will stop reading the customer and eventually lose its competitive position. However there is a certain vulnerability to approaching personal matters from this perspective.

One of the struggles most of us encounter along the path of balancing is in accepting the reality of newly defined situations. Intellectually, we have no problem, realizing that actions that brought fulfillment at one time may produce frustration and disappointment at a different period. However, responding to this intellectual glow of insight is a different story. As a young professor, my workaholic tendencies produced a level of publication and classroom engagement that was encouraged and rewarded by my organization. With few non-work commitments, a remarkably supportive spouse, and a small cadre of close friends, I found the pace and pattern of life I had chosen to be challenging yet reasonable. All of that changed when my oldest son was born. Although his birth had no effect on my work expectations (neither those externally nor internally imposed), other things did change. My wife needed more personal time. Her child-rearing activity meant that some of the tasks she had readily assumed needed to be "shared." (I offer this term guardedly as I would never presume that I came anywhere close to sharing home-focused duties and responsibilities with my wife). And not surprisingly, my son needed my time and attention. In short, my environment, my situation had changed precipitously.

Yet, I clung to the old situation that had brought me reinforcement, personal status and pride and a sense of security and acceptance. I refused to recognize that my situation was now quite different and that a continuation of old activity patterns would most likely lead to a depleted home environment, strained family relationships, and the lost capacity to be a strong, shaping influence in my son's young life. I'd like to say I figured this out early, but I did not.

I'll never forget the summer afternoon. Working in my home office was part of my "sacrifice" to leave the university office by mid-afternoon. Of course, nothing really changed but the setting, as I would retreat to my writing sanctuary. Engrossed in some relatively meaningless project that would

ultimately offer little or no important contribution to anyone or anything, I
was interrupted by an exuberant five-year-old who wanted me to come outside and play. My derisive and profanity-spiked reply shooed him from the
room, begging my forgiveness. But I will always be haunted by the look on
his face—a look of surprise, fear, disappointment—a look that indicated that
all his youthful, explosive excitement had just been ripped apart. The experience, now twenty years in the past, remains as one of the most embarrassing,
disgusting, and reprehensible acts of my life, compounded by the fact that the
one most affected was a child I professed to love and cherish.

This is a difficult story, but it was a wake-up call. It was a call to look at
my core and my purpose armed with new data; a call to rethink my situation
and my priorities; a call to recognize that part of the emptiness I was experiencing was due to the choices I was making, as well as the opportunities to
grow that I had refused to consider; a call that shouted that my self-centered
life orientation would never be appropriate or just or *meaningful*. Aside from
coming to terms with the evolving nature of life, the call in and of itself can
produce discomfort which is another stumbling block along the way.

Increased Discomfort

Unfortunately, knowledge of your core self and the identification of aspects
of your life situation that are out of alignment can lead to a heightened sense
of imbalance. If your life situation or environment does not match your core
gifts and purpose, you likely have a sense that you are blocked, stifled, or sub-
limated in some way. You may feel an increased nagging discomfort that once
was vaguely described as "out of balance," and now is known with some degree of certainty. Discomfort is easy to dismiss when there is no explanation
for it. But, once you label and define your gifts and purpose and become
aware of how your life situation fails to serve your purpose, discomfort becomes impossible to ignore.[18] Thus, we encourage you to keep pressing forward. Discomfort can become a catalyst for growth. Action is the only option.

Also, keep in mind that the receipt of feedback and information while balancing is not always a pleasant experience. Particularly in watershed moments, in which a decision will help to shape one's external situation to be
more or less in line with core self, it is important to remember that intense
emotion and reaction are not only normal, they are valuable. These signals
can be used as feedback and information to further define core self and act in
accordance with one's core.

Consider the following example. We recently coached a mid-level executive who was struggling with the prospect of an international assignment. Although he clearly understood the career significance of the assignment, he
lamented the family impact that the move would bring. Family concerns were

accentuated by his two high-school aged children and his wife, each of whom (for different reasons) shared strong preferences against a move. Importantly, now in his mid-forties, the executive realized that his decision took on a dimension of finality. Would such an attractive assignment be offered again? Would his decision signal company officers about his willingness to continue being the consummate team player? Would he be making a career-plauteauing decision by refusing the assignment? Any decision appeared to close some future options. And, not surprisingly, that awareness fueled his growing inner turmoil over this work-life issue.

Again, there is nothing wrong with this challenge and nothing wrong with the tension, anxiety and pain that the manager is experiencing. As we've mentioned, paying attention to these emotions (and even agonizing over the decision) is a psychologically healthy state. Realize that rather than single-mindedly following some other-prescribed career path, he has now allowed himself the permission to experience the pain (or trauma) of decision. He is assuming greater control over the range of possibilities for his life. And his search is peeling back layers of his core self.

How will he know whether his decision is right? How will he know if he has correctly identified the true, noble, heroic, and ultimate value and meaning of his existence? He will not. He makes the best decision today. And by doing so, he creates and moves incrementally closer toward his ultimate statement of meaning. He need not worry about choosing the "right" answer because there are many right answers. There are many ways to structure a life situation that engages our gifts and allows us to achieve our purpose.

Fallout

There is another reality of balancing that we devote the entire next chapter to discussing. However, it merits mention here that if you are like most of us, you have been living some combination of a life that is from your core and one that is expected or desired of you by others. This is expected, and healthy to some degree, as we all have responsibilities and roles we have committed to fulfill for others in our lives. But, whether you have been aware of it or not, acting from outside your core has built expectations on the part of others. Professional "others" may come to expect a certain level of commitment or focus that becomes more and more difficult once you realize your commitment is not coming from your core. As you begin to honor your core, particularly if you have not been doing so for some time, you will fail to meet some expectations of others. You will need to renegotiate working relationships and understandings. You may even breach trust.

To the degree you have internalized these expectations, you will also disappoint yourself. The self-disappointment stems from the natural grief process that must take place. One aspect of this process is letting go of the commitment and focus that you were demonstrating. Although you have realized that it does not serve you, letting anything go involves some degree of grief. After all, whatever you were doing served you well, and may have earned you the success you currently enjoy. Particularly if the purpose and gifts you are now expressing have been untested, it is natural to grieve the loss of something certain and safe. These and other storm flags that may be diminishing your view of new horizons are discussed in the next chapter.

ANOTHER LOOK BEFORE YOU LEAP

"I am cautiously optimistic about what you've said so far. Does this mean that all I have to do is to make sure I have activities in my life each and every day that tap my gifts and purpose?"

Absolutely, that is what this means. And, the more ways you tap into your gifts and purpose throughout the day, the greater sense of balance and meaning you will experience. The decision-making guidelines we have suggested help you maximize your potential to do this. By withdrawing from those roles and responsibilities that do not serve your core, and embracing those that do, you are more likely to garner life experiences that enable the expression of your core self.

Despite the strength of our conviction here, we must provide an answer that touches reality as fully as possible. Most jobs or activities are not unidimensional. They involve a series of tasks—some less fulfilling and stimulating than others. Yet, none can be ignored for overall success to be realized. In other words, a person with a creative, artistic core will not escape a morning of data analysis occasionally, and one who embraces data and structure will find herself in an excruciating brainstorming session on some fateful days.

So what does this mean as reality challenges our new-found sense of core self and acting to achieve its expression? We need reenergizing events and activities. These are purposely selected activities that more fully align with one's core, thereby offering a sort of counterweight to the "off-core" activities you must perform.

Accordingly, on days when you are pressed to engage in non-core activity for the majority of the day, it is important to reenergize by igniting the fire of your core self in some way. The "way" may not include your normal work regimen. And, counter to what is often the knee-jerk reaction, it may not involve pressing on, without interruption, until the sordid task is done. It may simply be some purposely built-in time to engage with what is at your core.

NOTES

1. The Greek "gnothi seauton" is inscribed in gold above the oracle in the city of Delphi, Greece. Although well-known and widely interpreted as a call to act upon self-knowledge, the author of the quote is unknown. It has been attributed to at least five ancient Greek sages, including Socrates and Pythagoras.

2. M. Scott Peck, *The Road Less Traveled: A New Psychology of Love, Traditional Values and Spiritual Growth* (New York: Touchstone, 2003), 64.

3. A study in the journal Hypertension has noted that adults who sleep less than five hours a night are more than twice as likely to exhibit high blood pressure as are those adults who sleep seven to eight hours. Quoted in Jennifer Barrett, "Slumber Party," *Newsweek* 147, no. 16 (April 17, 2006): 66.

4. Kate Sparks, Cary Cooper, Yitzhak Fried, and Arie Shirom, "The Effects of Hours of Work on Health: A Meta-Analytic Review," *Journal of Occupational & Organizational Psychology* 70, issue 4 (December, 1997): 391–408.

5. P. Buell and L. Breslow, "Mortality From Coronary Heart Disease in California Men Who Work Long Hours," *Journal of Chronic Diseases* 11 (1960): 615–26.

6. J. M. Harrington, "Shift Work and Health—A Critical Review of the Literature on Working Hours," *Annals of American Medicine (Singapore)* 23 (1994): 699–705.

7. J. Barton and S. Folkard, "The Responses of Day and Night Nurses to Their Work Schedules," *Journal of Occupational Psychology* 64 (1991): 207–18.

8. Noted in Sparks, Cooper, Fried, and Shirom, "The Effects of Hours of Work on Health: A Meta-Analytic Review," 391.

9. Many resources on work life balance forward this vague notion of down time, suggesting it is a period of rest or disengagement. We disagree, offering that it may well be a time of activity and engagement, but requiring the use of different gifts. Of course, this does not deny the importance of rest, but rather allows the individual focused upon "keeping busy" to recharge by breaking his or her personal pattern.

10. Reported in Jerry Adler, "In Search of the Spiritual," *Newsweek* (August 29— September 5, 2005):48.

11. Robert C. Fuller, *Spiritual But Not Religious: Understanding Unchurched America* (New York: Oxford University Press, 2001), 1.

12. It is interesting that this concept embraces a life-giving essence. Merrium Webster notes that spirit is from the Latin spiritus (literally, breath) and spirare (to breathe.) For a sound overview of a number of work-related perspectives, see R. A. Giacalone and C. L. Jurkiewicz, eds., *Handbook of Workplace Spirituality and Organizational Performance* (New York: M. E. Sharpe, 2003).

13. B. E. Ashforth and M. G. Pratt, "Institutionalized Spirituality: An Oxymoron?" in *Handbook of Workplace Spirituality and Organizational Performance*, ed. R. A. Giacalone and C. L. Jurkiewicz (New York: M. E. Sharpe, 2003).

14. Michael Argyle, *The Psychology of Happiness*, 2nd ed. (London: Taylor & Francis, 2001), 170.

15. Michael Argyle, *The Psychology of Happiness*, 164.

16. R. A. Witter. W. A. Stock, M. A. Okun, and M. J. Haring, "Religion and Subjective Well-Being in Adulthood: A Quantitative Synthesis," *Review of Religious Research* 26 (1985): 332–42.

17. A comment shared by hatha yoga teacher Brian Saeger while describing one aspect of his personal philosophy. Brian currently teaches in Boulder, Colorado.

18. This theme is consistent with the work on cognitive dissonance theory, which we have discussed previously. For example, see Festinger, *A Theory of Cognitive Dissonance*, 1957.

Chapter Eight

Storm Flags

Just recently, I spoke with Patrick, an individual I had coached through his own balancing process. Although he had never held an academic position, Patrick was a teacher at his core, inspiring others through his knowledge, expertise, and example. So, I was not surprised that after much deliberation, he had left a high-pressure sales position in order to manifest his gifts of communication, curiosity, and education in a philanthropic organization. This new career path brought special challenges, but challenges he willingly accepted as they were more in line with his core. Now, instead of asking others to buy, he would be asking others to give. At the outset, this was appealing to Patrick, a giving and nurturing individual himself. The position seemed to maximize his gifts while aligning nicely with his life's purpose, and he determined this next step on the path to balance was worth a relocation and reduction in salary.

Soon, I learned that while Patrick was enjoying the organization, his new residence, and several other aspects of his life situation, he was also feeling an intense disconnect between his role and his core self. While he was asking others to give, he did not feel firmly situated in his own desires to engage in selfless service. "I'm still asking for money," he shared. "And, I am so sick of that. But I uprooted my life for this position. I will let down the entire office if I ask for a change in job duties. And I have no idea what I should do next." Having just been through the state of groundlessness, he was hesitant to go there again. Understandably, he was exhausted, mentally and emotionally, still reeling from the trauma of his recent transitions. Stated simply, Patrick was in the midst of his own storm. Whether he chooses to make another change immediately or to build strength and courage by hunkering down in his current position remains to be seen. But clearly, Patrick is dealing with the intrapersonal storms that are a direct result of balancing.

After reading the previous chapter, you may find yourself exhilarated, ready for action, and comforted that there is a possible future for you that involves living from your core. You may also be a bit uneasy. Some of you are willing to admit this, but others may not. "This is great," the latter group of you thinks, "I know my core, and I am empowered to act upon this information. There's no reason to be cautious. Charge!"

Regardless of your emotional and psychological reactions to the work you've done to this point, you are about to be hovering between two trapeze bars. There will be a moment, sometime very soon, when you let go of the old and embrace the new, and in that moment, you will have nothing to hang on to. This sense of suspension, the awareness that there is no ground beneath your feet, produces discomfort that ultimately is borne of fear. All of us have been taught, particularly by our society, that fear is weak and not indicative of good leadership. However, we view fear as a normal, human response to change. It takes courage to make needed life changes, and even the most courageous among us do not act in the absence of fear.[1]

Thus, at the heart of our conversations on balancing is a subtle call to the courage and faith at your core. Even armed with the knowledge you have at this point, execution is not a foregone conclusion. In his book, *What About the Big Stuff*, Richard Carlson makes a critical analogy.[2] He notes that lions, having been caged for most of their lives, will refuse to leave the cage even when taken to an environment near perfect for a lion. The cage stands open, but the lion moves to the back of the cage and refuses any encouragement to come out. The fear of the unknown is often more powerful than the drain on psychic energy that living from outside of your core produces. The security of that to which we've been accustomed overpowers the discomfort and uncertainty of venturing beyond our established boundaries. Nova Knutson puts it best when she says, "Hint: The Cage is Not Locked."[3]

But fear is also the flag of awareness. We move only as fast and as far as we are capable. And we will only engage in change when the pain of immobility outstrips the pain of change. If fear limits your action, you have not yet experienced the numbing and debilitating impact of your current imbalance. Our hope is to offer enough ideas for your consideration that you are able to change without encountering and battling the pain. Yet, part of our humanness is a tendency to ignore these flags and push away our intellectual opportunities until something snaps—family, health, friendships, sanity, joy, life.

We truly believe that stepping outside of the cage, into a life situation that is more in line with your core, leads you toward a life of balance and meaning. Humans also change when there is the promise of joy, as pointed out in a 2005 Fast Company article called "Change or Die" by Alan Deutschman.[4] We also believe that many of the organizational, interpersonal, and intrapersonal ills in Western civilization are due to imbalanced lives. That is, when individuals choose to be who they think they "ought" to be rather than whom they were "meant" to be, each and every one of us (and ultimately our families and organizations) is shortchanged. And lastly, we know that some of the choices you will make are tough, and they are not without cost. Whether you have considered the cost of your actions explicitly or not, these inevitable casualties are the source of your subtle discomfort. In yet another paradox, it is the examination and active reconciliation of what is underneath that allows you to move forward. Yet, moving forward blindly is even more painful, if movement happens at all. We guide you through this period of honesty in this chapter.

In this chapter, we explore three types of storms that may arise as a direct result of your balancing choices and actions. Specifically, these storms may be intrapersonal, interpersonal, or organizational. You may experience severe hurricanes in one area, while only gentle spring rains fall in others. Or, you may find yourself in a severe weather warning in each of the three areas for the duration of your transitions. Your storm flags are unique and a direct result of your particular current life situation, your core self, and the gaps that exist between them. Just as in any storm, the only way out of it is through it. In addition to the guidance we provide, hopefully you will find additional guidance and support from those around you during what may be a challenging time. Above all, we need the courage to persevere. We are reminded of the words of Louisa May Alcott, "I am not afraid of storms for I am learning how to sail my ship."

INTRAPERSONAL STORMS

We are both intellectual and emotional beings. The tension between these two dimensions surfaces as we consider the changes that are prompted by inspired and honest balancing. Intellectually, you have been drawn to an understanding that patterns must be broken and that movement must occur. Still, the emotional energy and distress that surrounds the prospect of change can be overwhelming. It can also be stagnating. Accordingly, we must focus attention on the inner being that is being affected by the decision to gain better personal balance. The decision to act in accordance with one's purpose and gifts is pure and logical. But often this process involves personal change and transition, which carries with it as much grief, pain, and fear as it does excitement.

Grief

A few years ago, after considerable search and investigation, my family decided to move to the country from our home in an historical neighborhood. The new home was everything we had discussed and wanted—a three-acre wooded lot with seclusion and privacy, yet still only twenty minutes from our work. The weekend before our move, as we sat in the old house, I noticed my wife deep in thought with tears streaming down her cheeks. My inquiry into the problem led her to reveal that she had just been looking across the room at the oak-framed doorway leading from our family room to study. There on the frame were a series of vertical marks, almost notches of significance and progress. As you may have guessed, these were the marks of measurement of our two boys as they had aged from toddlers to teenagers. The scene was punctuated by my wife's commentary, "Those marks are my boys, and I remember the growth and pain and joy and sadness those marks represent." Then, came her stinging final conclusion, "After tomorrow, I'll never, ever see those marks again."

The scene has powerful metaphorical significance. Intellectually, my wife (and now, admittedly, I was feeling a bit sad too) understood and accepted the change that was about to take place. It made sense. It was what we wanted. It met or exceeded all criteria we had established. Yet, there were things that would never be the same, things we would never see again, omissions that would cause us pain and grief. We suggest that it is no different with the changes you are now contemplating. These changes will cause you to leave things behind. They will force you to break from patterns in novel and non-retractable ways. And these changes will produce, in many cases, levels of personal grief.

Grief is a puzzling emotion to confront and address. In fact, many people pretend to ignore their felt grief, forcing the emotion beneath the surface. Its effect, while submerged from immediate attention, is still dramatic and impactful. But why? Why do we ignore the reality and play an emotional game of "let's pretend?" Grief is an emotion for which hard-charging, success-oriented professionals have little time or energy. Further, we have no good patterns for how to encounter and handle the grief of change-driven loss.

The second aspect of grief involves grieving the entire time you spent living others' expectations rather than living from your core. We believe you will find that living from your core is a rewarding experience. You undoubtedly will wonder why you didn't know to do so, or allow yourself to do so sooner. Years or decades may have gone by caught up in trying to "balance" aspects of your life that are not life-giving, that are not from your core. You will have to forgive yourself for that, and grieve the lost time spent doing so.

Pain

A faithful companion of grief is pain. Fuller goes a step further and suggests that pain is a faithful companion of a life well-lived. He says, "to feel healthy and satisfied humans require not a tensionless state such as is provided by satiating our physical needs, but rather an active striving or struggling toward some worthy goal."[5]

While neither invited nor pleasant once it arrives, pain is an opportunity to make adjustments. We mistakenly live our lives in an attempt to avoid and escape from painful experiences. Of course, this makes sense. Most psychologically healthy adults do not search out or encourage avenues for experiencing pain. Yet, pain does arise. We cannot avoid it, nor should we be impervious to it. Likewise, while it is natural to find ways to abate the pain as quickly as possible, such actions are not always the most functional. Let us demonstrate this point. Philip Yancey has written extensively of his relationship with Dr. Paul Brand.[6] Brand, an accomplished and respected physician and surgeon, yielded a promising and lucrative career to work among lepers, arguably one of our most vilified and ignored populations. In engaging discourses on pain, Brand points out that lepers would gladly accept pain as it would change their entire existence. He notes that one of the effects of leprosy is that the afflicted person's nerve endings are destroyed so that the pain sensation cannot be realized. Accordingly, a leper may rub his leg persistently, producing the large sores often identified with the condition, precisely because there is no pain to tell him to stop. We view the pain of change in this way. It is a signal to stop, take stock of what is happening, and choose a purposive (i.e., core-driven) course of action.

Note that we are not advocating that one wallow in pain. We are advocating that one allow the experience of pain to be a prompting or awareness that critical decisions are looming. They cannot and should not be approached with a cavalier attitude. And they must not be brushed aside, dismissed, or assuaged simply to reduce the pain.

Fear

There is one more emotional force at work here. Change, particularly personal behavioral change, frequently generates another powerful emotion — fear. Understanding, recognizing, and admitting this emotional reaction as an intrapersonal storm is critical. Fear often shakes us to our core and leads to uncertainty and self-doubt. Questions of identity and capability arise that haven't surfaced in years. We wonder, "Will I be able to do what is required?" "Will I be as effective, as competent, as respected as I embark on and practice new behaviors?" "Will I have to give up too many of the things that have brought others to view me positively?" Our fears, our fears of ineptitude, our fears of loss of status, our fears of the unknown, and our fears of uncertainty clamor for attention and urge us to hold on and maintain the status quo. At

times, these fears overwhelm and block our movement even as we intellectually grasp the importance of the change. To a large extent, fear is the culprit.

Let's press a bit more deeply on this point. We have a need for all the pieces
to fit together. We don't like the disparate tugs and strains of competing demands. We want to service it all. We want all the pieces of life to align in a
consistent and consonant way. This desire for cognitive consistency is fundamental. There is an idealized perfect equilibrium that drives our emotions and
energies. We will accept some deviations or dissonance from true consistency. In fact, we have a threshold of dissonance that we can accept and manage. However, when the breaches of balance push beyond this threshold, we
are shaken and disrupted. We sense a loss of control. And we feel threatened.
Whether we choose to admit it or not, we experience fear—a fear that things
are getting out of hand, a fear that we are losing control.

Dissonance wrapped in fear becomes an intriguing motivator—what we refer to as an aversive motivator.[7] In short, we are driven or motivated to take
action to avoid or eliminate the aversive condition and return to that acceptable threshold, that level of assumed consonance. But for some, fear becomes
a destructive force. It can produce stagnation, trauma, and confusion that im-
mobilize our needed response. Thus for some, fear becomes a great motivator; for others, fear is the great immobilizer.

So what does all this mean? Stepping in balance uncovers pain and uncertainty. It also strips us bare to the experience of grief. Yet, we can approach
these emotional expressions with healthful attitudes. As we've stated repeat-
edly, the first step in this healthy approach is admitting two things: the emotions are real and the emotions have an impact. Accordingly, one needs to admit the reality of the emotions rather than ignoring or suppressing their
existence. Emotions that are dealt with directly can be cathartic, informative,
and transformative; emotions that are not addressed seethe beneath the surface and influence us in indirect yet powerful ways. Critically, over time, un-
expressed emotions do not cease having an effect. Rather, at some point, we
become victims of their unexpected release.

The second step is to understand that the emotions, however deep and
wrenching, are typical and natural. We are not aberrant or maladjusted for
feeling pain, fear, and uncertainty in the face of life-altering change. The
aberration would be a void of pain, fear, and uncertainty during a time of loss,
disarray, and transition.

One of the key functions we serve as executive coaches is to legitimize the
emotions of those we coach. When we do, we are often met with sighs of relief. We believe the sighs are a release of the stress associated with harboring
what were perceived to be, just moments before, non-productive and "weak"
emotions. Realize that these emotions arise from your core, the place of your

values, purpose, and gifts. Emotions are a vehicle to your meaning, not an obstacle in your path. In fact, the origin of the word "emotion" is the Latin, "emovere," which means "to move."[8]

The third step is to garner the courage to progress through the grief and pain rather than being immobilized and thwarted by its uncomfortable presence. When one acknowledges emotion that has heretofore been unrecognized, a natural reaction for some is to feel victimized and aggrieved. In many cases, victims of their emotions lead stagnant lives. Victims are passive and fretful. It is understandable why these subtle emotions would produce paralysis rather than progress. It is ultimately imperative to realize that while you have little control over emotions, you have ultimate control over your behaviors. Emotions are springboards for action. To use psychological terms, self-efficacy, rather than self-esteem, is paramount in this situation. While the self-esteem argument leads us to believe we will act better when we feel better, the self-efficacy argument promises that core-inspired action is the means to satisfaction. As noted by psychologist O. H. Mowrer, "It is easier to act oneself to a better way of feeling than to feel oneself to a better way of acting."[9]

As if reconciling and confronting these emotions were not enough, ultimately balancing also means you must confront a new you. Most of us have a reasonable sense of self, a subjective appraisal, known as our self-concept.[10] Even with its flaws and warts, at least we recognize the existing self. We have, in all likelihood, learned how to handle ourselves, both in regards to our self and others, to compensate and excuse the deficiencies we see. However, balancing creates a new self, replete with unfamiliar actions, emotions, assumptions, and expectations. You must confront that new self even as that self appears dramatically different from the person you have known for years. Although a new engaged and balanced self must surface and meet the outer world of family, friends, and work associates, the first and toughest force you have to face is yourself.

Our advice here is twofold, and while simple to give, it is much more difficult to execute. First, make time to get to know your core self in the new life situation you have created. Of course, this entire book has been about exploring that core self and coaxing it to the surface, but once it sees the light of day, you may have even more to discover and consider. That is, once you interact with family, coworkers, and others from a different "center," you may learn of additional aspects of your core. For instance, upon careful exploration of my own core, I found that there was an incredibly creative, yet somewhat messy aspect to who I was. This had been suppressed, though, by pressures to be good and "together" and by an admittedly perfectionist approach to life. Once unearthing the gift of creativity, and putting it into play in the way I lived, it became less and less possible to view myself as perfect. All of this work was internal, but it also set into motion a chain of events that allowed me to see others as creative, yet imperfect beings as well. My own ridiculously high expectations of and impossible standards for others gave way to compassion and acceptance. As I learned to live from the creativity at my core, more and more aspects of my core revealed themselves. I needed to "get to know" these aspects and how they would play out in my life experience.

Many of the techniques to do this have already been described in chapter five of this book, as they involve paying attention to the data that is all around you. Just as the example illustrates, your task now is to realize that you still have worlds to discover within; paying attention doesn't stop once the core self is activated.

Second, practice acceptance. Treat yourself as you would your best friend. If a loved one came to you, grieving and fearful over some recent loss, you would give that person kind words and your presence. You would not hold that person to a pre-loss standard of behavior or productivity. Rather, you would allow the person to find a new ground beneath his or her feet. Do the same for yourself. Even if the emotions have passed, you may be in a new situation with new surroundings, new people, and new tasks. It took a long time to become comfortable with the previous life situation; it will take time to become comfortable with those aspects that have changed. If you were giving advice to your son or daughter in this situation, what would you say? Something accepting and encouraging, right? Do the same for yourself.

Intrapersonal storms are sometimes turbulent and challenging to the core in and of themselves, but they also can be both the cause and effect of two other types of tumults that are the result of balancing: interpersonal storms, in which relationships with family and friends are thrown into flux, and organizational storms, in which your place within the organization is no longer clear or well-defined. We discuss these issues next.

INTERPERSONAL STORMS

It goes without saying that balancing affects the interpersonal domain of our lives, sometimes profoundly. One of the key interpersonal constituents to be affected is the family. In many cases, our high regard for family and our intent not to disappoint family members conflicts with our desires to move in new directions with our core self in the driver's seat. Finely tuned family dynamics may be thrown into disarray. Understandably, family members can experience confusion and may express rebellion. An entire realm of behavioral study, known as family systems theory, addresses the intricate and complicated web of interactions that are now being disrupted.[11] This does not mean that family members lack understanding or support. On their part, they are dealing with two forces. First, family members are trying to understand the new person (you) that they see evolving before them. Second, they are trying to evaluate and formulate how they will be affected and how they will have to adjust. Remember, from our discussions above, how difficult it was to reconcile this for yourself; imagine what it may be like for others who do not have full information about where you are and how you came to be there.

By way of personal example, I remember a spring day a few years ago when I escaped to my parents' home for some rest and relaxation. I was lying in a hammock, reading, while my mother was doing some gardening a few yards away. We had been sharing space comfortably for about an hour when she approached. "Jennifer, I feel as if I've lost you. Do you even have goals in your life any more?" I remember feeling angry at first. I was right there, in a hammock, in her backyard! She hadn't lost me. But, she had. I had. In a period of concentrated transformation, I was rebuilding who I believed myself to be using all of the information I had about who I was at my core. She was also correct that I didn't have goals. Not in the traditional sense, at least. And this was quite the change for her little girl who declared her double major the first week her freshman year and planned for graduate school two full years in advance. My first (and only) priority at that time was to discover what kinds of goals would be appropriate for all I was discovering within. My actions were frightening to her. She was not at my side through this intensely personal journey, and she had no idea what that meant for her in her role as my mother.

As this example shows, family members may have a visceral reaction to your choice to live more from a core purpose and set of gifts. The family is where one's emotional life is nurtured. Joy and pain are shared, as are strength and vulnerability. The patterns of behavior to nurture this emotional life, whether in a couple or in a family, may have also developed from a non-core place. That is, these patterns may have evolved from societal views or extended family histories. In my case, a family value was stability. Decisions were forever, and it meant a personal failure if any one of us was not happy and content with the life borne of our decisions. As a general rule, we did not communicate about doubts, yearnings, and dreams.

If these patterns are not congruent with a newfound sense of purpose and gifts, change must occur. And, like altering or breaking one silk thread of a spider web, the entire structure of the family may change. At the very least, each family member will feel the reverberations from altering just that one thread. To complete the example, my family still does not understand entirely when I engage in activities that are completely counter to the life I have created for myself through my own decisions. They didn't "get it" when I resigned my faculty position and moved to California, and they didn't "get it" when I moved back to the Midwest, all because it felt like the right thing to do. At my core, I thrive on variety and challenge much more than I do stability. I am happy to report that though my family members don't understand it, through communication and mutual respect, they've come to both expect and accept it.

Perhaps surprisingly, though, changes in the behavior and outlook of loved ones are not the most difficult piece. Often it is more fundamental. The transformational process that takes place when shifting the locus of expectation from external to internal is an isolating time; it involves introspection and individuation from others. The process can be threatening, as it is often difficult to communicate the nature of this shift. Family members who have been there for one another through the most challenging of times may feel helpless and unwelcome. Thus, the family clearly pays a price for this process of reflection and revelation. But, the individual is also paying a price, one of not being understood, which leads to further isolation and introspection.

> We were having coffee one morning with a young professional who had recently learned that her company had been restructured. She used this time to make a decision to exit the career she did not find personally rewarding, although her next career move was sketchy at best. She struggled with her options, which were plentiful, but none of her options allowed her to move closer to her life partner. She was having a hard time communicating with him, but instead of helping her through her ambiguous struggle, he focused upon what was easier to understand, and he continually pressured her to move closer to him. What he did not know was that she had been searching for jobs in his area, but none of them were resonating with her as being in line with her purpose and gifts. As she was recounting the situation, she stopped and said, "We could make this career change about us, but he seems only to be interested in making it about him. My only option is to make it about me."

She was experiencing the interpersonal fallout from making decisions in line with her core. Again, when decisions have not been made from the core for some time, the fallout from doing so can be particularly stressful and consuming. However, we cannot emphasize this point enough: there are many, many sets of external circumstances that allow us to live from our core. Sometimes, aspects of the core conflict with one another. It is no coincidence that we lament work-life balance. At times, being a parent conflicts with being an executive. The key is to use information and feedback from serving both aspects of the core to find the situations that bring these two into harmony. Each choice helps you more closely approximate the ideal manifestation of these two aspects of your core. Particularly when others are involved, be they family members or professional contacts, communication and honesty are in order. In the case of the young professional, both partners moved to the West coast to embark upon new careers that resonated with each of them. They are now married, and have found themselves in the midst of external circumstances that they contend are in balance.

Before moving forward, and in order to help you weather these interpersonal storms, we want to spend some time discussing honest communications. First, it is important to understand that the reactions of loved ones are human—their concern is benevolent, their "fight or flight" response is adaptive, and they are experiencing a combination of grief, pain, and fear (albeit indirectly) as discussed above. While this may strike you as an oversimplified explanation, consider for a moment that most people experience interpersonal conflict when their expectations, their hopes and dreams, are thwarted in some way. As you go about the process of balancing, you are essentially critically examining and sometimes dismantling expectations you have of yourself. The expectations most at risk of demolition are those that are linked to a non-core existence. We stand by our encouragement to engage in this process. But, we also recognize that family members and close friends are going to feel this acutely. In fact, they may experience it on two fronts.

First, to the extent that your behavior has become expected, it is a beacon of safety and security, a touchstone in the often demanding and chaotic world outside the home. Even behavior that is not core-driven—coming home later than expected due to stresses and strains from a position that does not utilize your gifts, setting unrealistic standards for your family reflective of the standards that were set for you, or locking yourself into the role of provider and disciplinarian despite your strengths in connecting with others—are known entities. We often warn managers that even when making positive changes like becoming more open and honest with feedback, they may be met with confusion and backlash. The operative word here is not "positive." It is "changes." As we've discussed, change is often met with resistance and resistance is a product of undesired grief, pain, and fear.

Secondly, to the extent that your life situation is intertwined with those of your family members, there are dashed expectations about lifestyle, income, geographic location, and the like. A vision of the future is a powerful thing. Even though it has not occurred, we cling to it as fervently as we do our current reality, if not more so. Realize that before any aspect of this vision actually changes, it is human nature to grieve the loss of an expected future.

Amidst thwarted expectations, keep in mind that there is another disruptive force at work. By your actions, you may also be trumping the natural process by which people become familiar with and eventually embrace change. At a fairly advanced point in your process of paying attention, learning of your core, and considering changes in your life situation, you will explicitly bring it to the attention of those around you. Even though your emotional decision to change has been evolving for some time, those around you are in only the awareness stages. They will need to move through several additional stages including investigation and reflection before adapting to, let alone embracing, change that has become a forgone conclusion on your end.

Thus, it is important to remember that you are bringing in completely new information, and significant others will respond accordingly. They will be surprised. They will be shocked. They will be disappointed. They will be hell-bent to change your mind back to the way it was. In some cases the significant others in your life will be emotional and confrontational. In other cases, they will be dismissive and pouty. In either case, their intent, at times subconsciously, is to stop the impending change and the havoc it may wreak on their current and future life situation.

An analogy may be helpful here. Organizational experts often cite "boiled frog syndrome" as a warning to leaders to scan the environment lest they be caught off guard by incremental changes.[12] My insightful undergraduates often use the same example to explain resistance to change. The biological survival mechanisms of frogs detect large shifts in environmental conditions; frogs cannot pick up subtle, small cues. Therefore, a frog placed in a pot of boiling water will jump out, over and over again, in an attempt to survive. A frog placed in room temperature water that is slowly brought to a boil, though, will remain in the pot the entire time. Unfortunately, in this analogy, you are the boiled frog! Your personal insights and internal changes have been incremental and comfortable. On the other hand, once expressed, your new ideas and views may be shocking to your family members. To survive, they will move out of the way, and quickly, particularly if they have not noticed the subtle cues you have been sending. Unless you have involved significant others heavily to this point, it is likely you will receive some reaction that smacks of resistance to change.

At this point in the book, you know us well enough to anticipate what we will be suggesting. It is pretty clear to you that we will be asking you to communicate, and that communication will involve self-disclosure. While revealing one's true self can be extremely liberating, it also requires you to accept some measure of vulnerability. We know, all too well, that more vulnerability is likely not appealing to you right now. In fact, the prospect of opening an already tender or raw place to others may cause you to close down even more tightly. While we encourage you to honor your human tendencies, we also implore you to summon the courage to move ahead, engaging in the necessary interpersonal exchanges. Do so consciously, though. We will offer a road map of sorts to help you have these difficult, but essential discussions.

Begin by discussing the reality of the situation, your roles and responsibilities, your relationships, and your life path. Often times at the outset of such discussions, we skip over these more mundane details; we assume our significant others know them already, and our desire to express discovery and hope is much more powerful. Although it may seem pedantic, taking the time to begin with reality helps to provide context for what you are about to unleash. It is a way to help others glimpse the path of development you have been experiencing and living. Discussing reality anchors your evolution in something firm and factual, which can be a grounding force in the face of impending change. It respectfully slows the process down in order to honor the natural adaptation to change process that others are only just beginning to confront. Discussing reality also shows that you are aware of, and have considered, the life situation you share. What can potentially be seen as a time of "all about me," becomes much more palatable if you take the time to acknowledge the "us" aspect of your shared life situation.

Once the reality has been discussed, engage in an open and honest discussion of your balancing journey. What brought you here? Was it an event? An emotion? What prompted your journey to explore your core self? What did you find at that core? Your gifts? Your purpose? What did you discover about mixed messages along the way? And, what do you feel these new discoveries will call you to do?

At this point, we must offer a practical caveat. While it is all fine and dandy to openly talk about and share mixed messages and actions, there is a devil in those details. These communications can degenerate very easily into a blame game. It is important, before going any further in your discussions, to work through any blame that may arise. Realize that at the outset, it is helpful for you to have made peace with how you arrived at your current life situation before engaging in this type of communication. A trusted friend or counselor may be helpful here. But even if you have arrived at a place of peace, communicating that to others is no easy task. Significant others love and care about you, and it will be natural for them to shoulder some of the blame if you find yourself in a dissatisfying and imbalanced life situation and they may respond defensively. It would not be unreasonable to hear in response, "I never told you that you had to be a doctor! I could pursue my art without your income!" Realizing the humanness of these types of reactions, understanding them, communicating honestly about your thought processes, and summoning the wherewithal and grace to keep communicating in the face of reactions (positive and negative) are important. We cannot stress enough that in the midst of your own transformation, the strength to keep communicating may not be easily accessed. In this case, seek help from a counselor, friend, or advisor.

The conversation can then proceed to a discussion of the overall impact of your balancing process and your initial thoughts about action steps. As you may expect, this is a process rooted in your unique partnership and history together. It involves negotiation and understanding. And, it also may call upon your gifts and purpose. Recognizing your purpose as it relates to family and significant others helps to shape your choices about how to fulfill your purpose professionally.

Much needs to be discussed, and it often stretches beyond the course of one conversation. Don't miss this point. Pacing your disclosures, particularly if they will involve major life changes, is important. Communicating more than the other party is capable of hearing, digesting, and supporting, is not only wasted effort, but effort that produces frustration and fractured attention for the listener. Whether over two conversations or ten conversations, it is at this point that you will discuss life choices and their impact. How will these choices affect the family? What roles and responsibilities can receive less of your time and attention? What roles and responsibilities do you foresee receiving more of your time and attention? What current and future goals and expectations need altered? Are there others that need to be involved in the process?

Once again, we have led you to a place of optimism that does not come free of the cost of reality and responsibility. There are not interpersonal fields of daisies among intrapersonal and organizational storms. There are challenges here, and they are formidable. We urge you to communicate, honestly and openly. We encourage you to keep communicating, even when it is painful and tense. We implore you to accept some vulnerability as the price of freeing self-disclosure. And, we ask you to seek help if needed As if two storms were not enough, we present you with a third and final type of discord that may arise from the process of balancing: organizational storms.

ORGANIZATIONAL STORMS

In the proceeding sections, we have addressed some of the personal and interpersonal fallout that accompanies balancing decisions. In this section, we turn our attention to organizationally-related outcomes that often arise when core-based balancing decisions are made.

Probably the most damning piece of organizational fallout is the way one is valued or revalued as personal balancing decisions are put into practice. As we've discussed in chapter three, even within organizations that express life balance as a basic corporate value, behavioral expectations frequently do not support what is espoused. Companies that include family concerns as core organizational values often are corporate pressure cookers. Here, all-consuming enterprise perspectives are strongly encouraged and richly rewarded, generally through favorable performance reviews and advancement opportunities. These double-bind messages, espousing one set of values and rewarding another, are prevalent and disheartening. In many organizations, for example, long hours of work are assumed to be competitive necessities for aggressive, upwardly-bound professionals who battle for limited slots of advancement. Thus, one's personal balancing efforts may result in organizational decision makers rethinking whether the proper corporate fast-tracker attitudes and actions are really present.

One promising manager related to us his quest for a corporate vice presidency. Walking by the desk of a colleague one day, he observed a pad of paper with half a dozen names, one with a line through it. Inquiring about the names, the manager was told that these names represented his fellow manager's competition for the next VP opening. The scratched name was a high potential manager who had turned down a foreign assignment because of the untimely stress it would place on his family. And accordingly, he was no longer a competitive threat. We would be naïve to ignore that advancement costs, such as this, may be associated with balancing choices.

There is a further complication. Associates, much like family and loved ones, often do not know what to make of carefully thought out balancing choices. We worked with a talented computer systems expert in his mid-thirties. He and his wife, also a talented professional in the marketing field, struggled with how to advance their careers while giving critical developmental time and attention to their two pre-school-aged children. After many soul-searching discussions, the couple decided that the husband's skill set made him considerably more flexible in his career. Consequently, they decided that she would pursue her career in the traditional 8-6 model, while he stayed at home, cared for the kids, and worked as much as possible from his home. The birth of "Mr. Mom" broke every stereotype and pattern his employer (an upstart software company) had cherished. Why, the employer reasoned, would a talented, young professional sacrifice his career potential in such a dramatic way?

Admittedly shaken by the organizational response, this professional maintained his commitment to yield corporate "face time" for "family time," a decision that no doubt cost him a promotion and a fast-track up the executive ladder. Yet, as a family, goals and boundaries had been established. He recognized that his role as nurturing parent was every bit as critical and meaningful as the organizational growth he had temporarily put on hold.

At times, personal balancing decisions create considerable organizational uncertainty and disruption. For example, we worked with a hands-on CEO who decided, after a life-threatening health battle, that adjustments in his career and corporate thinking had to occur. His personal crisis had led him to believe that he needed more time for self, family, and recuperative relaxation.

"That's what led me to a new company structure that's going to take me out of operations . . . I really need to spend more time with the children and actually this is going to be much better for the customers as well. . . . The reason I explain this is because through personal analysis . . . (I realize that I) don't have to work until I drop from exhaustion."

Of course, such a decision, logical and reasonable as it was, posed major changes for the company. The CEO conducted a series of mini-retreats to help the leadership of the business redefine roles, direction, and strategic approach—all from the perspective of engaging the CEO in long-run visioning and strategy but removing him from most direct operational involvement.

The previous conversation has discussed role adjustment, but at times, zeroing-in on core self prompts one to engage in balancing considerations that result in either changing companies or changing careers. Both changes are extreme moves that should be taken only when the evidence shows a clear misalignment of core self and organizational demands with no reasonable prospect for remediation. Commonly, people have tried (perhaps for years) to find stop-gap changes that will render major organizational and career breaks unnecessary. However, as a last resort, these extreme changes may be the healthiest option.

One senior manager described to us a change that he had made seven years earlier, moving from one highly regarded company to another. He noted that his assignment with the new company required that he work longer hours and in more intense settings with both internal and external customers than he had done with his previous employer. Yet, he noted that he loved the new assignments, which more directly tapped his talents and creativity. Accordingly, he experienced an energizing dimension to his new job rather than the depletive frustration he encountered in his previous position.

There are no easy answers to any of the organizational issues we have raised. They require straightforward communication similar to that described previously in the interpersonal realm. Yet, there is an added complexity since the communication between organizational colleagues typically lacks the depth, understanding, and emotional commitment that are shared with family and friends. There is much more room for misinterpretation. Further, to express the depth of one's core self opens a range of personal exposure and vulnerability that is generally absent in corporate encounters. Self-disclosure is frequently viewed with suspicion and puzzlement.

Honest, direct, eyeball-to-eyeball encounters are needed. Sharing honest emotion and affirming behavioral intention are the approach. Both themes must be included. Modifying behavioral intention (and thereby expectations) without including the driving emotions will be hard for others to understand. However, presenting strong emotive arguments without the accompanying intentions leaves the listener searching for direction and clarity. The pieces must progress hand-in-hand.

Let's look at an example of how this occurs. A participant shared with us his decision to step off the corporate managerial track and return to the professional pool. Recognizing the potential impact of the decision, he arranged to have face-to-face exchanges with his boss, each of his managerial peers (seven in all), and each of his direct reports. In each session, he shared the reasons for his decision, his impression of what this would mean for his role in the division, and how he felt the division could and should respond. He was open to questions, input, and suggestions. Yet, he adhered, unfalteringly, to his personal value boundaries that included less administration, lower levels of stress, and more family and personal time. Importantly, he was receptive to any argument that embraced these boundaries, even when it took him in a new or unexpected direction. Eventually, what emerged was a new organizational role that engaged his talents creatively for the organization, while allowing him to be honest to his newly experienced core self.

We've taken you through these storms because they are part of the balancing landscape. Tumultuous as they are, the conversations outlined in this chapter must occur. A life created devoid of resolving these internal and external conflicts directly is not a life in balance at all. It is a life of disappointment, because you have now glimpsed the core self but have not worked through the painful steps needed to obtain the meaning and balance that is now possible. Lest the allure of meaning has faded while considering the difficulties that may arise in obtaining it, we take one last opportunity to discuss the crux of balance. Next, we discuss meaning.

ANOTHER LOOK BEFORE YOU LEAP

"I've tried to have the changing life/core self discussion with my spouse. It didn't go over well. I found myself pulling back and second guessing myself. What's wrong?"

Nothing is wrong. First, your spouse may be offering you valuable information and perspective that has not been fully considered. It needs to be. It may mean more reflection on your part. Or, it may signal that your reflecting needs outside input in order to run its course. Either way, your conviction is probably not as strong as you thought. That's good data. Work with it, refine it, and the result will be a stronger resolve to honor your emerging core self.

Second, as we've noted in this chapter, it's all new information for your spouse. While the spouse may have noted signals and drawn interpretations, you have now confirmed that something is up. You have raised these concerns to a prominent and undeniable level. At this point, its easy for a spouse to attribute your new spirit of self to job stress, your religious conviction, that pesky mid-life crisis, or any number of plausible explanations. Let's not immediately focus on the merit of these varied explanations. Rather, step back and recognize where your spouse is—a vulnerable place where he or she needs more time, communication, understanding, and patience. While your sense of who you are undergoes transformation, the role others play in your life inevitably transforms as well. We do not move and change in isolation.

NOTES

1. We are reminded of a quotation from the great Mark Twain: "Courage is resistance to fear, mastery of fear–not absence of fear."

2. From Richard Carlson, *What About the Big Stuff?* (New York, NY: Hyperion Books, 2002).

3. As quoted in *Meditations from the Mat* by Rolf Gates and Katrina Kenison (New York, NY: Anchor Books, 2002).

4. A. Deutschman, "Change or Die," *Fast Company* 94, (May 2005): 52–62.

5. Robert C. Fuller, *Religion and the Life Cycle* (Philadelphia: Fotress Press, 1988), 69.

6. See Paul Brand and Philip Yancey, *The Gift of Pain* (Grand Rapids, MI: Zondervan, 1997); and Philip Yancey, *Where is God When It Hurts?* (Grand Rapids, MI: Zondervan, 1990).

7. See Leon A. Festinger, *A Theory of Cognitive Dissonance* (Evanston, IL: Row, Peterson, 1957).

8. The Latin stem "mot" serves as the root of the words "move" and "emotion."

9. As quoted in *Meditations from the Mat* by Rolf Gates and Katrina Kenison (New York, NY: Anchor Books, 2002).

10. Self-concept can be defined as the behaviors, characteristics, and roles one deems typical of himself or herself. See B. M. Byrne, *Measuring the self-concept across the life span: Issues and instrumentation.* (Washington, DC: American Psychological Association, 1996)

11. Leslie B. Hammer, Margaret B. Neal, Jason T. Newsom, Krista J. Brockwood, and Can L. Colton, "A Longitudinal Study of the Effects of Dual-Earner Couples' Utilization of Family-Friendly Workplace Supports on Work and Family Outcomes," *Journal of Applied Psychology*, 90, issue 4 (July, 2005): 799–810.

12. Popularized by Peter Senge in his book *The Fifth Discipline* (New York, NY: Currency, 1990).

Chapter Nine

At the End of the Day . . .
There is Meaning

Kent was a young manager in his early 30s. We were struck by the honest, soul searching intensity of our coaching encounter. Having earned six promotions in seven years, Kent's range of responsibilities had increased exponentially. His managerial success had led his company to broaden his span of control to include 25 direct reports. He was the embodiment of the adage that "if you want something done, give it to a busy person." Needless to say, within a year, the demands began to exact their toll. Experiencing stress-induced, physiological reactions to his work and life responsibilities, Kent knew that a significant life change was necessary. During our conversation, it was apparent that Kent had investigated his core self; he had ideas about his gifts and purpose that he felt could guide his impending life change. With additional family responsibilities of a new child, the commitment to spend quality time with his family and the clear realization that his personal health could no longer be ignored, Kent strategized about how to make necessary career adjustments. Collectively, we concluded that Kent would meet with his immediate manager and ask for relief, even if that meant moving off the managerial fast track. Kent even shared that he knew family and personal issues had to take priority over his career aspirations. Admittedly, Kent knew this would be a difficult decision to put in place. He shared that part of his sense of self (our words, not his) came from the success, achievement, and importance garnered from his career. He left our meeting with a clear plan and scheduled a meeting with his boss to set his plan in motion.

One week later, we again met. Kent's demeanor had changed dramatically. Confusion and distress were replaced with confidence and good humor. He smiled as he approached, and we looked forward to his recount of a successful conversation that would bring him closer to living in line with his core self. We were further intrigued when he said, "I've got it all figured out." He then expressed that the meeting could not have gone better. He explained his situation, his boss was understanding, and his boss was responsive. Kent beamed as he indicated, "They gave me a promotion, fewer direct reports, greater opportunity in the organization, and a 20% salary increase on top of it all. You guys are great. It only took one good coaching session."

Our encounter with Kent was revealing. In many ways, his reflections and balancing activities are the story of this book. At the same time, Kent's situation reveals the complexity, struggle, and uncertainty that surround balancing and finding meaning. Each of us wants it to be resolved, to be "figured out." Each of us wants and needs the comfort and clarity of closure. And, yet, each of us is usually willing to take the path of least resistance, to stop moving toward the fullest expression of our core selves in favor of yielding to a simpler solution. At these crossroads, we would rather be "finished" than "complete."

Using Kent's story as our backdrop, let's review where we have been. An underlying goal of this book has been to help you uncover, examine, and express your core self. We recognize from experience and research that this depth of realization is likely prompted by adversity, fear, or crisis in your life. However, be it adversity or enlightened proactivity that has brought you here, we hope that through the process of reading and reflecting, you have recognized and appreciated your individuality, your uniqueness, the talents and gifts and purpose that are inimitable because they are solely yours. We have stressed that living apart from or in conflict with this core will lead to ultimate frustration, tension, and that indefinable feeling that life is just not what it should or could be. In turn, from a purely personal perspective, living from one's core brings satisfaction, joy, and the potential for meaning.

Although redundant, we again must emphasize that there is no route to balance and meaning that short-circuits the process of honest, in-depth self reflection. This book has railed against the onslaught of simplified, quick-fix, formulaic approaches. While these approaches may ameliorate the symptoms of imbalance by serving our need for action, they do not address that which is beneath the surface. They do not address our deeper psychological, emotional, and spiritual selves.

Going back to our example, Kent began this arduous process of honest personal reflection; he was eager to resolve his troubling family and health situations by tapping into his core. At the outset, he seemed less interested in a quick-fix, and truly dedicated to using his current adversities as a launch point for more significant life change. He planned for action, action that included difficult conversations and life-altering decisions. But then, something happened.

His process of balancing took an unexpected turn. Unpredictably (although completely consistent with corporate culture and practice), Kent's company responded to his plight by offering a promotion. Having prepared himself for resistance, inner unrest, and conflict when approaching his boss, Kent was met with praise and adulation. Accordingly, rather than removing himself from the chain of managerial progression as he had planned, Kent stepped up another notch, becoming further entrenched in the pattern that had proven so destructive.

Kent has made a call and he has taken action. Will that action yield better balance and deeper meaning? Or is Kent simply deluding himself again by diverting his focus to additional job commitments? On the surface, it seems Kent is moving away from his core and even ignoring some of the critical boundary conditions of his life. At this point, you may be waiting for our resounding "Wrong!" to be showered upon Kent. Actually, "wrong" is not the case at all. Short term, Kent's decisions may be problematic; they may exacerbate problems that already exist and create new problems to be handled. Long term, however, Kent's trend line is positive. He's done some reflection, made a decision, and is currently seeing the beginnings of the outcome. If he pays attention, and reflects upon the effect of these actions, he will be better served when the next watershed moment presents itself.

Living from gifts, particularly in the beginning, is not a predictable life. It is one of trial and error, where the match between gifts and situations is tested over and over again. Some of those tests will result in experiencing meaning; others will not. But, one gets to know both. Something is missing, or it is not; something is meaningful, or it is not. We tend to shy away from the trial, in order to avoid the risk inherent in the error. Of course, the risk is that of disappointment, of experiencing a lack of meaning. Even these experiences are valuable, though, in that they are guideposts to what does *not* work. The next action, the next choice is better informed and better capable of producing meaning.

Kent's example also reminds us of the power of external forces and mixed messages. Despite his thoughtful determination, Kent's course of action was swayed by organizational opportunity and expectation. His established behavior and accompanying sense of contribution were reinforced and fueled by the challenges offered him. Rather than honoring his newly discovered core self, he was lured into a behavioral pattern that had heretofore produced reward . . . and also discomfort. Again, realize that Kent's being influenced is not necessarily wrong or right. All we know for sure is that he was influenced. Only Kent can determine if the organizational enticements reflected a new part of his true core self, or if they deflected his attention from his core self. Perhaps he can make that determination now, if he honestly reflects, or perhaps the nature of his decision will reveal itself over time. Regardless of Kent's ultimate path to balance, it is important to realize how susceptible each of us is to the mixed messages of significant others. Once accessed, it is imperative that the core self be kept at top of mind awareness, so that mixed messages lose some of their false allure.

AT THE END OF THE DAY

There are two responsibilities to living a life in balance. The first is to engage in the personal reflection necessary for identifying, accepting, and embracing one's core self. We have spent the bulk of our efforts in this book on this dimension of life balance. We have presented the process of personal reflection and awareness as both fundamental and pivotal for finding balance and subsequent meaning. Garnering this knowledge is a key accomplishment in and of itself; most people do not have a sense of their gifts and purpose. But knowledge alone is not enough.

There is a second, corollary responsibility that must move hand-in-hand with the revealed core self. This is the responsibility to express the core self. As we have already noted, expression requires courage. Often, there are pressures and pushback that serve to stagnate or lead expression astray. Regardless, we must keep in mind that aligning one's life situation with gifts and purpose, through modification or creation, is the route to core expression. But it is a route with no endpoint. Alignment is an ongoing task. Expression is the life's work we call balancing.

It is not lost on our reader, particularly one who has made it this far, that the expression of core self is to some extent inner-focused. It involves one's awareness of and commitment to "taking care of oneself." Yet, there is an additional dimension of meaning that you cannot disregard. One's expression of core self must engage an outer-focus, an other-focus, if meaning is to extend beyond self-indulgence.

Do not fear that we are changing our tune now that you have reached the last chapter. Our main point still stands. If you are looking outside yourself for what you seek in terms of balance or meaning, you will not find it. That being said, you must look and act outside yourself in order to obtain full and ultimate meaning.

There are two reasons for this. One, you have external obligations and responsibilities that are other-focused and non-negotiable. These obligations must be accepted and fulfilled whether they arrived in your life through living from your core or not. For example, you may have an obligation of parenthood. While your core self may contain gifts and purpose in line with organizational leadership, your obligation to your family is non-negotiable.

Therefore, your career will need to find expression in a manner that allows you to maintain your parental obligations. To relegate parental obligations in favor of satisfying one aspect of your core produces the friction and discomfort most people label as imbalance. The challenge is to find an outlet for both, perhaps bringing to bear the same gifts of leadership in your role as a parent. The tension experienced when denying other-focused obligations finds us further away from, not closer to, balance.

The second reason you must maintain a degree of other-focus is that meaning is derived through your connection to, impact upon, and support of other people. Most major philosophic and theological perspectives of life's meaning rely on this other-focus, offering that one's deepest and most powerful calling evolves as we shift focus from ourselves. Understand that without a sense of core to guide us in these interactions, we don't have a chance. Thus, awareness of core self is a necessary but not sufficient condition for finding a life of meaning.

As is apparent by now, touching other individuals in some core-aligned way is fundamental to our humanity and essential to our deepest experience of meaning. Recognize the duality in this statement. Core-alignment is individual, but self-indulgent when it stands alone. Reaching out is other-focused, but self-denying when it stands alone. As you reconcile these two foci and discover core-alignment *through* reaching out, meaning is enhanced.

At the end of the day . . . the search for meaning must be created and experienced. As Webster reminds us, meaning is a hidden or special significance. In this game of hide and seek, one may search many hiding spots before he or she finds the hidden. But this active search is much more effective and more rewarding than remaining at the counting spot, hoping for some profound revelation or rationalizing and analyzing where the hidden may be found.

We brought you to this point, primed for the experience of meaning. We have discussed the likely hiding places, we have warned of the distractions and false leads, and we have described for you the powerful experience of discovering that which you seek. But do not mistake this point for the finish line where you are guaranteed the medal of meaning. Meaning requires action. It requires breaking patterns and stepping into the realm of uncertainty. It requires taking a step because meaning dictates we do so, even when the immediate path is slippery and unsure. It requires faith that the core self you have found will steer you aright. As you close this book, what will your next step be?

Appendix

This book is largely a book of personal reflection. Accordingly, readers have asked us to help and guide them on their path of reflection. Included here are additional thought starters, questions, and exercises that aim to spark additional thinking about the very personal and idiosyncratic aspects of balance in your life. This section is not meant to be an exhaustive set of critical issues. Rather, it is intended to stimulate your thinking and help you probe the often neglected domain of your core self. These questions may even be conversation starters for significant others or colleagues. As with the rest of the material in this book, we offer this appendix as an alternative way of viewing balance from which you are invited to select those ideas that resonate with you.

CHAPTER ONE

- What brings you to this book? Why did it catch your eye on the bookstore shelf? What are you hoping to accomplish through reading it? While the comments and path put forth in the book guide you in a specific direction, you will find that our suggested path to balance encourages you to bring your own concerns and goals to the table. Two people reading the same material may find different aspects helpful, or may be launched in different directions even though reading the same words.

We invite you to set an intention at this point. Intentions are different than goals. Where goals are specific and objective, intentions are general and subjective. When accomplishing a goal, there is a particular end state we hope to achieve. We can check it off the list as "done." For example, we may set a goal to reach Boston by Tuesday. We know when we've arrived in Boston and we know if we've done it by Tuesday without question.

When pursuing an intention, we move in a relatively consistent direction, but allow ourselves to explore and veer off course as additional information is taken in. We may set an intention to travel northeast. In this case, we may reach Boston, but we may also decide that Virginia Beach is worth exploring a bit along the way. In both cases, we are successfully pursuing the same intention.

With that in mind, what is your direction? Set an intention here. As I read this book, I will pay particular attention to:

- Expectations are powerful forces. Often we don't even realize that we are holding expectations, but when expectations are dashed, we often experience disappointment and frustration. Not only do unmet expectations show us that we had expectations in the first place, they also show us where we are stuck. Identifying expectations can illuminate the sources of our current frustration. In this case, they may tell us something about the sources of our frustration as we seek the elusive balance.

How is the material that is included in the first chapter different from what you expected based upon your own notions of balance or other books you may have read on the topic? Is it possible that your expectations are a signal about the places you may be stuck in during your search for balance?

CHAPTER TWO

- What is the nature of the organizational pressures you are experiencing? Are there efforts toward cost-cutting, efficiency, and/or growth that contribute to your personal sense of imbalance? How widely shared is this felt pressure? Has pressure given way to a sense of loss or personal minimization, either for you or those around you?
- Examine your assumptions about career success as it relates to such things as work hours, accomplishments, and career paths. Where did these assumptions come from? And, more importantly, what impact have they had upon your sense of success and balance?
- Are you a victim of "when this project is over" thinking? Has your work history supported the reasonableness of this trap? In other words, have things ever slowed down for any substantial period of time after finishing a large project?

- Referring to the compensatory nature of some individuals' escape to work as a remedy for imbalance, have you found refuge in working more in the hopes that one day balance will be your reward?
- Observe yourself in the course of one week. When striking up a conversation with others (and being asked some version of the inevitable "tell me about yourself" question), how prominent are your work roles in your response? Your non-work roles? What are your personal aspirations in each? Which of your beliefs are healthy, life-giving responses to your various roles and responsibilities? Which are unreasonable and unattainable?

CHAPTER THREE

- Who are the important significant others in your life? Those whose opinions you seek out and value? Realizing that being honest about the messages they may be sending does not diminish your feelings about them, what signals do they send about the choices you are making in your life? How have your life choices and/or your emotions been affected by these messages?
- Disengaging for a moment from all external messages and signals, attempt to verbalize your standards, your definition of success, your definition of a life well-lived. How are your standards different from those put forth by society or significant others in your life?
- With whom do you typically compare yourself? As an exploratory exercise, take a moment to shift your comparison to someone with whom you do not typically compare yourself. How does your demeanor change when you make this shift? Sometimes physical posture even changes. We may sit taller when we feel "greater than" or slump in our chairs when we feel "less than." Do this as many times as necessary such that you understand both the power and the folly of using such a standard to bestow value judgments.
- How do you want others to see you? Is this dramatically different from who you are? If so, how do your behaviors attempt to hide your true self in favor of the self you wish others to see and appreciate? Remember that there is a difference between privacy and secrecy. While privacy is healthy, secrecy leads to the sublimation of our true selves and the pursuit of a life that can only lead to imbalance.
- How has your ability to be connected to your workplace helped or hindered your work/life balance? If you do not have a good idea of how much time you spend working away from work, we invite you to log your hours in order to get a more accurate assessment of the effects of connectivity.

CHAPTER FOUR

- Have you engaged in the "grand juggling assignment," segmenting time and energy into the various facets and roles in your life in the hopes that this will help you obtain balance? If so, what were the results? Are you more or less balanced having engaged in such an activity?
- Examine your assumptions about balance. Do you have hopes that one day you will obtain balance, once and for all? Do you seek balance as an end state, or do you accept it as a moving target? When you speak to others (e.g., coworkers, family members, friends), what language do you use? How are the words you choose indicative of your assumptions?
- We have all wished for more time at one point or another. Think for a moment about how much extra time you would need and what you would do with that time. For instance, you may determine you need 4 extra hours in each day in order to read business books and magazines and to spend with your children. Whatever activities you find in this exercise are clear indications that these aspects of your life are important, but not receiving the time they deserve. Think creatively about how to serve these aspects given the 24 hours per day you do have. For instance, can you listen to books on CD during your commute? Can you devote dinner time to family?
- Think of a time you have experienced negative spillover. Now, think of a time you have experienced positive spillover. Do these concepts resonate with your life-balance situation? Can you reconceptualize your experience in the integrative terms described in the chapter, and then use this information to create more positive and less negative spillover?
- What "a-ha!" experiences did you have when considering that balance may be about meaning rather than juggling, problem-solving, or time? How can these realizations help you in your quest for balance?

CHAPTER FIVE

- Are you currently experiencing the adverse effects of imbalance? Has imbalance affected you physically and emotionally? Or, has imbalance negatively affected your relationships? If you have arrived at a point of examination due to adversity, your experience will likely be much different from that of the individual who is taking a more proactive approach. Perhaps surprisingly, there are advantages and disadvantages to each path.

For those in the midst of adversity, there is an urgency and priority to your balancing efforts that will keep you sustained and focused. However, there may be uncertainties within or undesirable aspects of your current life situation that may act as obstacles as you move through your balancing process.

For those proactively seeking balance, you have arrived at this point before any major crisis or irreversible damage in your life situation. However, it will be easier to slip back into old patterns and to discount some of the more difficult work you will be asked to do as you reflect and create a life of balance.

Take inventory for a moment. Given your reasons for pursuing balance, what is your motivation? Your sense of urgency? What are the aspects of your life situation that may hinder clear thinking and concentration (e.g., illness, divorce)? We often find that acknowledging that which may trip you up in your process allows you to better anticipate these stumbling blocks and obstacles. Anticipation, in turn, allows you to determine a way to meet them head on, rather than falling victim to circumstance. Take a moment to plan for meeting these obstacles when they arise in your quest.

- How do you define imbalance? Does this description come easily to you? More easily than a description of balance may have before reading this book? We also invite you to ask colleagues and friends to describe both imbalance and balance. We were fascinated by the responses we received in our interviews. We think you'll find the results interesting at the very least and meaningful conversation starters at best!
- What are your personal cues of imbalance? How does imbalance show up in your life in the form of inner emotional tension, moodiness, myopic focus, frustration, or physiological responses? When these cues arise, what immediate actions do you take to reduce the associated tension?

CHAPTER SIX

- Defining purpose is probably the most challenging introspective exercise we will ask you to do in this book. It is complex and shaped by life events and experiences. Paradoxically, though, it is simple and transcendent of the many roles and responsibilities each of us hold. It is a question that, if allowed, will haunt you over the next few weeks and months as you look for evidence and explanation of your life's purpose. Your purpose is much more likely to present itself, though, if you are working from some grounded place. Purpose rarely appears out of air. In very practical terms, this means that a "draft" statement of purpose will evolve, while general thoughts on purpose will likely lead to confusion and frustration.

Two exercises may help you on this quest. In the first, think briefly about the themes that run through those aspects of your life in which you feel the most at home. Are you a caregiver at home, at work, and with extended family and friends? Are you a motivator and challenger? Are you a thoughtful visionary? If you can identify one or two themes, jot them down and set an intention to observe yourself and your relationships over the next few days and weeks. In this observation, the initial statement can be refined and honed.

Some people find it more difficult to define what purpose is, but they clearly have an idea of what it is not. This "back door" method is another means to ascertain the first few strains of purpose. Begin by asking yourself what your purpose is not, what aspects of life grind against your sense of who you are? Once identified, ask yourself why this is so. The answer to the second question is likely evidence of your purpose. Several examples of this exercise appear in chapter seven.

• Identifying gifts is typically an easier exercise, but one that is no less important in your quest for balance. In fact, you may be able to pinpoint two or three gifts without engaging in much reflection. If we are lucky, significant others and good leaders have given us feedback about those things we do better than anyone. These comments, particularly if they keep surfacing again and again, are evidence of our unique contribution and potential. Owning our gifts, believing the kind words of others, is often the greatest challenge in these situations.

There is another exercise in which we often ask workshop participants to engage that helps to refine and uncover gifts. On a sheet of paper, take a moment to make a list of five roles in which you have been a success. These can be work roles or non-work roles, current roles or past roles. Once you have your list of five, create another list along side. This time, list WHAT has made you a success in these roles. This list will likely be longer, and many of the characteristics you list will overlap multiple roles. For instance, your keen observational skills may make you a successful parent and a successful industrial engineer. Lastly, place a star next to those characteristics that show up again and again, in multiple roles. These are your gifts.

The exercise works because we are often recognized, promoted, and praised for those things we do well. We are then offered positions and experiences based upon these characteristics, which offers us more practice in these areas. Practice, of course, is the polish that makes these characteristics even stronger and more brilliant. You can see the cycle. People recognize our gifts, put us in positions to use them, which makes us even better in those areas, which leads to more recognition, and on and on.

- Once you are aware of your unique gifts, the next thing we'd ask would be to identify those places in your life where they are being used. What is the impact of this? By impact, we mean, how does that affect you? And, how does it affect others? It is important that you identify the impact, as this is your touchstone, your signal that you are on the right track. As we will discuss in the next chapter, the goal in creating balance is to use your gifts as often as possible. The impact, psychological and relational, is an important indicator that you are doing so.
- What gifts are you not using? Are there gifts that either have gone unnoticed or unutilized in your life? When you think of these personal characteristics, what do you experience? A sense of loss, frustration, or grief? Feelings similar to the feelings you have identified as imbalance?
- In what ways have your purpose and gifts evolved? That is, what have you become? Perhaps gifts have deepened, or perhaps they have shifted all together. Purpose may be fairly stable, but different aspects of purpose may have been discovered or taken on new significance over time. Think back to one or two ways your core self has evolved over the course of your lifetime in order to personalize the concept of being and becoming.

CHAPTER SEVEN

- What is your experience of the fundamental balance dilemma? That is, what emotions, thoughts, and inner experiences arise as you identify and accept the disconnections between your core self and your life situation? Realize that whatever you are experiencing is most likely normal and most certainly human. Acknowledge your inner experience, but remain open to working through it toward a state that is more apt to produce decisions that are proactive rather than reactive.
- Take an inventory of your physical, mental, and spiritual boundaries. What do you need in each of these areas? (For instance, how much sleep do you *need* each night? How often do you need to reflect and refresh? What are your outlets for spirituality and how often must they be served?) For each of these, it is important to be as accurate as possible as to your *needs*. Even though you may have been getting by with six hours of sleep per night, are you at your best the next day? Does seven or eight hours ensure a more life-giving day?

The next question is, are you currently operating within these boundaries? If not, your first step toward balancing will be to make shifts to bring your life situation more in line with these boundary conditions. Playing within bounds is a necessary condition for balance. Just as you cannot score a goal if you are out of bounds, you cannot live a life in balance if you are violating your personal, human needs. What actions are necessary to begin living within healthy boundaries?

- Define your value boundaries as well. Complete the sentence: "In order to live a life in balance, I will not sacrifice. . . ." Again, if any of these value boundaries are currently being violated, you cannot move further along the path of balance. What actions are necessary to adequately serve those aspects noted in the sentence completion?
- Several exercises designed to help you make decisions about roles and responsibilities that will bring you balance were outlined in chapter eight. They are replicated here for convenience.

First, begin by listing the roles and responsibilities in your life situation. Be sure to capture the richness of these roles. You may be a daughter, but that role is influenced by the geographic proximity of your parents, their health, and the ways in which they wish to be a part of your life. While it may become apparent in this process how your roles either do or do not allow for the expression of your core self, this is not our initial focus. Save those thoughts, but do not allow them to detract from your inventory of your life situation.

Once your roles and responsibilities are laid out in front of you, you may be aware of several things. The first reaction is often a reaction to the quantity. We are often unaware of how many important roles we fill, and we are often unaware of the nuances that make them unique and different from the experiences of others. Your second reaction will likely reveal itself when you take the next step, which is to evaluate each of your roles and responsibilities against your core self and purpose.

Begin by listing your gifts and purpose down the left hand side of your notebook, journal, or spreadsheet. List your roles and responsibilities across the top. Then, for each role, place a mark in the row if the role taps into that particular gift or purpose.

	Role 1	Role 2	. . .	Role 12
Purpose 1				
Purpose 2				
Gift 1				
Gift 2				
. . .				
Gift 8				

We encourage you to devise a system that works for you. You may place an "x" in the column if that role fully taps a gift, but a "√" if it only partially does so. You may also know that in the near future, one of your roles will no longer serve the purpose it once did; this scenario may involve some other notation. Try to carry out the entire process of evaluation with some degree of objectivity and equanimity. Emotions and concerns will undoubtedly surface. While we encourage you to acknowledge them and perhaps even stop the process to consider them deeply, do not allow them to guide any decision-making until you have had time to view the entire picture of your roles and responsibilities. Also, following such an introspective exercise, we recommend avoiding action for a period of time to allow your discoveries to sink in. There will be plenty of time to take action and adjust any findings that trouble you.

There are some additional questions to ask yourself as you consider your findings. It is important to view the entire landscape of your life situation and ask yourself: Are each of my gifts being served in some way? Are there gifts that are not being served? Are there roles that are redundant? Are there roles that are serving few if any gifts?

• How do your findings map to the four balancing quadrants? Specifically, which roles and responsibilities will you embrace and nurture? From which must you withdraw and/or release? Which must be added? Basic goal setting techniques and action planning will help you here. Ask yourself, what specific actions are necessary for each of these roles and responsibilities? Which actions take priority? What is the most logical sequence of action? At which points will you recalibrate your balance journey by updating and reevaluating your personal balance grid? Finally, how will you hold yourself accountable for taking these crucial balancing steps?

As with any action planning and goal setting process, each of us will respond best under different conditions. For some, writing or typing the action plan and keeping a physical copy in a visible place is necessary. For others, recruiting friends and family to provide accountability and support is necessary. For yet another group, the process of goal setting is enough to allow us to more intuitively chart our course; we may never look at our notes again. We cannot stress enough the importance of utilizing the process and technique that works for you. If you are having trouble identifying this process, we urge you to look to your own reflections for guidance. What are your gifts? How can you use your gifts to create balance?

• Think for a moment as to how you will navigate the stumbling blocks of balancing. How will you ensure you are allowing for your own evolution?

How will you handle the increased discomfort you will likely experience in a way that keeps you moving toward balance rather than a way that continues to hold you back?

CHAPTER EIGHT

To some extent, the content of this chapter does not apply universally. That is, the fallout we've described will impact each of us differently, and it will unfold as you engage in balancing. There is very little for which you can plan and prevent. That being said, some questions may help you become vigilant in recognizing fallout when it occurs, and understanding it as it unfolds.

- What is your personal experience of change? How do you respond as your environment changes, either due to actions within your control or outside of your control? What emotions, thoughts, and inner experiences arise? More importantly, how have you dealt with these reactions? Has your approach been effective? If not, how can you alter your approach to more effectively handle the certain emotions that arise due to your life changes?
- What conversations must you have as you engage in balancing activities? In preparation for these conversations, consider aspects of timing and the personality of the others involved in the dialogue. In what ways will your conversations lead to a deepened intimacy? In what ways will your conversations breach trust? Lastly (but importantly), who are your external resources as you navigate these interpersonal responsibilities? Who are the trusted advisors, counselors, or clergy that you can enlist?
- What organizational fallout is likely from your actions? Given your knowledge of the organization, its leaders, and its history in handling similar issues, how will your actions be received? How will you be revalued as a leader, an associate, and as a loyal employee? How do you suppose you will respond to fallout from the organization? What preemptive steps can you take?

CHAPTER NINE

- On your journey toward balance, what will your next step be?

LaVergne, TN USA
26 September 2010
198523LV00002B/32/P